Cheek by Jowl

Cheek by Jowl

by

Ursula K. Le Guin

Seattle

Aqueduct Press, PO Box 95787
Seattle, WA 98145-2787
www.aqueductpress.com

Library of Congress Control Number: 2009923617

Publication Acknowledgments: Previous publications are noted at the beginning of each essay.

Cover: Details from a painting by an unknown artist from Guerrero, Mexico: Collection of Ursula K. Le Guin

Cover and Book Design by Kathryn Wilham
See list of illustrations on page 136.

ISBN: 978-1-933500-27-0

10 9 8 7 6 5 4 3 2 1
This book was typeset in Jenson Recut.
Printed in the USA by Thompson-Shore, Inc., Dexter, MI

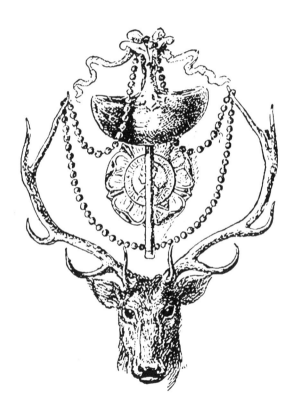

Contents

Some Assumptions about Fantasy

This talk was written for the Children's Literature Breakfast of the big professional book fair, Book Expo America, in Chicago on June 4, 2004. Some bits were cannibalised from the longer piece, "The Young Adult in the YA."

IT seems very strange to me to fly 4000 miles to speak for ten minutes at breakfast. To me breakfast is when you don't speak. At most you grunt. Nothing more than that should be required. I wish I could just grunt at you in a friendly, polite way that meant "Thank you all for being wonderful people who bring children's books to children!" and then sit down among a chorus of moderately appreciative grunts. However.

It was suggested that I tell you things like how I create children's books and why, and how my books are part of my life. That is exactly the kind of subject that I can't even grunt about. I don't know anything about how or why, only about what.

So, what are my books for kids and young adults? All but one of them are fantasies, including the new one, so I will grunt about fantasy.

Some assumptions are commonly made about fantasy that bother me. These assumptions may be made by the author, or by the packagers of the book, or both, and they bother me both as a writer and as a reader of fantasy. They involve who the characters are, when and where they are, and what they do. Put crudely, it's like this: in fantasy, (1) the characters are white; (2) they live sort of in the middle ages; and (3), they're fighting in a battle between good and evil.

Assumption I: The characters are white. Even when they aren't white in the text, they are white on the cover. I know, you don't have to tell me about sales! I have fought many cover departments on this issue, and mostly lost. But please consider that "what sells" or "doesn't sell" can be a self-fulfilling prophecy. If black kids, Hispanics, Indians (both eastern and western), don't buy fantasy, which they mostly don't, could it be because they never see themselves on the cover?

I have received letters that broke my heart, from adolescents of color in this country and in England, telling me that when they realised that Ged and the other Archipelagans in the Earthsea books are not white people, they felt included in the world of literary and movie fantasy *for the first time*. Worth thinking about?

Assumption 2: Fantasy Land is the middle ages. It isn't. It's an alternate world, outside our history, and its map isn't on our map. It may resemble mediaeval Europe in being pre-industrial—but that doesn't justify its having no economics and no social justice. Nor does it explain why nobody there ever feeds or waters their horses, which run all day and night just like a Prius. The best send-up ever of this fifth-hand Tennyson setting is Monty Python's *Holy Grail*, where horses are replaced with coconuts. Whenever I find a fantasy that is set in a genuinely imagined society and culture instead of this lazy-minded, recycled hokum, I feel like setting off fireworks.

Assumption 3: Fantasy by definition concerns a battle between Good and Evil. This is the cliché the cover copy writers love.

There are lots of fantasies about the Battle between Good and Evil (the BBGE), sure. In them, you can tell the Good guys from the Evil guys by their white hats, or their white teeth, but not by what they do. They all behave exactly alike, with mindless and incessant violence, until the

Problem of Evil is solved in a final orgy of savagery and a win for the Good team.

Many fantasy movies and most interactive games go in for the BBGE, which partly explains the assumption that books do the same. And it's true that in fantasy, character is often less important than role (also true of Greek tragedy and much of Shakespeare, where role and character can be almost, if never quite, the same thing). Carelessly read, such stark stuff may appear to be morally simplistic, black-and-white. Carelessly written, that's what it is. But careless reading of carefully written fantasy will not only miss nuance, it will miss the whole nature and quality of the work.

This has happened over and over to *The Lord of the Rings*—it has been carelessly read, through the dark glass of assumption and prejudice, and so misread as a simplistic morality tale. Even in the film version, where, though Tolkien's plot is followed faithfully and the Ring is destroyed, the focus on violent action and the interminable battle scenes overshadow and fatally reduce the moral complexity and originality of the book, the mystery at its heart.

As for my stuff, how or why anybody could call it a battle between Good and Evil is beyond me. I don't write about battles or wars at all. It seems to me that what I write about—like most novelists—is people making mistakes and people—other people or the same people—trying to prevent or correct those mistakes while inevitably making more mistakes.

Immature people (of any age) crave and demand moral certainty: This is bad, this is good. Kids and adolescents struggle to find a sure moral foothold in this bewildering world; they long to feel they're on the winning side, or at least a member of the team. To them, heroic fantasy may offer a vision of moral clarity. Unfortunately, the pretended Battle Between (unquestioned) Good and (unexamined) Evil obscures instead of clarifying, serving as a mere excuse for violence — as brainless, useless, and base as aggressive war in the real world.

I hope that teenagers find the real heroic fantasies, like Tolkien's. I know such fantasies continue to be written. And I hope the publishers and packagers and promoters and sellers of fantasy honor them as such. While fantasy can indeed be mere escapism, wish-fulfillment, indulgence in empty heroics and brainless violence, it isn't so by definition — and shouldn't be treated as if it were.

Fantasy is a literature particularly useful for embodying and examining the real difference between good and evil. In an America where our reality may seem to have been degraded to posturing patriotism and self-righteous brutality, imaginative literature continues to question what heroism is, to examine the roots of power, and to offer moral alternatives. Imagination is the instrument of ethics. There are many metaphors beside battle, many choices besides war, and most ways of doing right do not, in fact, involve killing anybody. Fantasy is good at thinking about those other ways. Could we assume, for a change, that it does so?

The Wilderness Within

This piece has been altered slightly from its original appearance in the second edition of *Mirror, Mirror on the Wall: Women Writers Explore their Favorite Fairy Tales,* edited by Kate Bernheimer (Anchor Books, 1998). It was printed also in my collection, *The Wave in the Mind,* Shambhala, 2004.

INFLUENCE—the anxiety of influence—I've come to dread the well-intended question, "What writer or writers influenced you as a writer?"

What writer or writers didn't? How can I name Woolf or Dickens or Tolstoy or Shelley without implying that a hundred, a thousand other "influences" didn't matter?

I evade: telling the questioners they really don't want to hear about my compulsive-reading disorder, or changing the playing field— "Schubert and Beethoven and Springsteen have had a great influence on my writing"—or, "Well, that would take all night, but I'll tell you what I'm reading right now," an answer I learned from being asked the question. A useful question— *What are you reading right now?*—which leads to conversation.

Then there was the book, *The Anxiety of Influence.*[1] Yes, I know who's afraid of Virginia Woolf. Still I'm faintly incredulous when I hear that phrase used seriously. The book came out at the same time that a lot of us were energetically rejoicing in the rediscovery and reprinting of earlier woman writers, the rich inheritance that had been withheld from all writers by the macho literary canon. While these guys were over there being paranoid about influence, we were over here celebrating it.

If acknowledging the influence of great writers makes some authors feel threatened, what about *fairy tales?* That should bring on an regular panic attack.

That the accepted notion of literary influence is appallingly simplistic is shown, I think, by the fact that it overlooks, ignores, disdains the effect of "pre-literature"—oral stories, folk tales, fairy tales, picture books—on the tender mind of the pre-writer.

Of course, such deep imprints may be harder to trace than the effect of reading a novel or a poem in one's teens or twenties. The person affected may not be conscious of such early influences, overlaid and obscured by everything learned since. A tale we heard at four years old may have a deep and abiding effect on our mind and spirit, but we aren't likely to be clearly aware of it as adults—unless asked to think about it seriously. And if seriousness is limited to discourse on canonical Literature, we might well be embarrassed to mention something that was read to us after we'd got into bed in our jammies with a few stuffed animals.

I have absolutely no idea of when I first heard or read the tale of the Sleeping Beauty. I don't even remember (as I do for some stories) the illustrations, or the language, of a certain edition. I certainly read it for myself as a child in several collections, and again in various forms when I was reading aloud to my own children. One of those versions was a charming Czech-made book, an early example of the Pop-Up genre; it was good magic, the way the thorny rose-hedge leapt up around the little paper castle. And at the end everybody in the castle woke, just as they ought to, and got right up off the page. But when did I first learn that that was what they ought to do?

The Sleeping Beauty, then, is one of the stories that I've "always known," just as it's one of the stories that "we all know." Are not such stories part of our literary inheritance? Do they not influence us? Does that make us anxious?

In any case, we *don't* know the stories we think we've always known. I checked out the Sleeping Beauty tale and found that I had most of it pretty clear: the happy christening feast for the new baby Princess, to which all the local fairies are invited, and each gives the baby a gift—beauty, wealth, good nature, etc. But a fairy who didn't get an invitation arrives in an understandable snit and gives the baby a very backhanded gift: if she should ever prick her finger with a spindle, a certain doom will fall upon the castle. So no spinning is allowed in the castle, and the baby grows up beautiful, wealthy, good-natured, and entirely ignorant of the nature of spindles. Therefore, when one somehow comes into her hands, she pricks her thumb with it (not, actually, an easy thing to do with a spindle). At that moment everybody in the castle and its environs falls into a deep sleep, and a tremendous hedge of thorns grows up all around. The sleep will last until a prince wakens the princess with a kiss. Source versions of the story in France and Italy include various baroque complications after the prince arrives, but as I knew it, as most Americans know it, the story ends with the prince's kiss and everybody getting ready for the wedding.

And I wasn't aware that it held any particular meaning or fascination for me, that it had "had any influence" on me, until, along in my sixties, I came on Sylvia Townsend Warner's evocation of the tale in a tiny poem (it is in her *Collected Poems*):

> The Sleeping Beauty woke:
> The spit began to turn,
> The woodmen cleared the brake,
> The gardener mowed the lawn.

> Woe's me! And must one kiss
> Revoke the silent house, the birdsong wilderness?[2]

As poetry will do, those words took me far beyond themselves, straight through the hedge of thorns, into the secret place.

For all its sweet brevity, the question asked in the last two lines is a total "revisioning" of the story, a subversion of it. Almost, it revokes it.

The pall of sleep that lies upon the house and grounds is supposedly the effect of a malicious spell, a curse; the prince's kiss that breaks the spell is supposed to provide a happy ending. Townsend Warner asks, was it a curse after all? The thorn-hedge broken, the cooks growling at their porridge-pots, the peasants laboring again at their sowing or harvesting, the cat leaping upon the mouse, Father yawning and scratching his head, Mother jumping up sure that the servants have been misbehaving while she was asleep, Beauty staring in some confusion at the smiling young man who is going to carry her off and make her a wife—Everything back to normal, everyday, commonplace, ordinary life. The silence, the peace, the magic—gone.

Really, it is a grand, deep question the poet asks. It takes me into the story as no Freudian or Jungian or Bettelheimian reduction of it does. It lets me see what *I* think the story is about.

I think the story is about that still center: "the silent house, the birdsong wilderness."

That is the image we retain. The unmoving smoke above the chimney top. The spindle fallen from the motionless hand. The cat asleep near the sleeping mouse. No noise, no bustle, no busyness. Utter peace. Nothing moving but the slow subtle growth of the thorn bushes, ever thicker and higher about the boundary, and the birds who fly over the high hedge, singing, and pass on.

It is the secret garden; it is Eden; it is the dream of utter, sunlit safety; it is the changeless kingdom.

Childhood, yes. Celibacy, virginity, yes. A glimpse of adolescence: a place hidden in the heart and mind of a girl of twelve or fifteen. There she is alone, all by herself, content, and nobody knows her. She is thinking: *Don't wake me. Don't know me. Let me be...*

At the same time she is probably shouting out of the windows of other corners of her being, *Here I am, do come, oh do hurry up and come!* And she lets down her hair, and the prince comes thundering up, and they get married, and the world goes on. Which it wouldn't do if she stayed in the hidden corner and renounced love marriage childbearing motherhood and all that.

But at least she had a little while by herself, in the house that was hers, the garden of silence. Too many Beauties never even know there is such a place.

Sylvia Townsend Warner's lines haunted my mind for some while before I realised that her question had led me not only into the folktale of the Sleeping Beauty but into a story I had to write about it. In this case, the influence was almost direct. I am not anxious about it in any way. I am cheerfully grateful.

My story is called "The Poacher" (it is in the collection *Unlocking the Air*). Its title describes exactly what I, the author, was doing: poaching on the folktale's domain.

Trespassing, thieving. Hunting. Tracking down something that happened in the place where nothing happens.

In my story a peasant boy lives at the edge of a forest where he poaches and gathers a very poor living for himself, a nasty father, and a gentle stepmother. (I find reversing stereotypes a simple but inexhaustible pleasure.) The stepmother is not much older than he is, and there is a sexual yearning between them that can find no solace. He discovers the great hedge where it cuts across a far part of the forest. This impenetrable, thorny, living wall fascinates him. He keeps going back to it, exploring along it. When he realises that it forms a circle, a complete defense of something within it, some *other place*, he resolves to get through it.

As we know from the tale, the magic hedge is yards thick, yards high, and regrows two razor-thorned shoots for every one you cut, so anybody trying to get through it gives up pretty soon. The uninvited fairy's spell decreed that it would stand for a hundred years. Only when the hundred years are up will a certain prince appear with a certain sword, which will cut through the monstrous tangle like a hot knife through butter.

Our peasant boy doesn't know that, of course. He doesn't really know anything. He is dirt poor and ignorant. He has no way out of his life. There is no way out of his life. He starts trying to cut through the hedge.

And he keeps it up for years, with the poor tools he has, slowly, slowly defeating the ever-regrowing vitality of the thorn trees, pushing a narrow, choked opening through the trunks and branches and endless shoots and tangles, doggedly returning and returning; until at last he gets through.

He does not break the spell, as the prince will. He has broken out of his life, *into* the spell. He has entered it.

It is not he who will revoke it. Instead, he will do what the prince cannot do. He will enjoy it.

He wanders about the fields and gardens inside the great hedge wall, and sees the bee sleeping on the flower, and the sheep and cattle sleeping, and the guardians asleep by the gate. He enters the castle (for in the tale as I knew it, Beauty's father is the king of the realm). He wanders among the sleeping people. My poacher says then, "I knew already that they were all asleep. It was very strange, and I thought I should be afraid; but I could not feel any fear." He says, "I knew I trespassed, but I could not see the harm."

He's hungry, as he has been all his life. "The venison pastry that the chief cook had just taken out of the oven smelled so delicious that hungry flesh could not endure it. I arranged the chief cook in a more comfortable position on the slate floor of the kitchen, with his hat crumpled up for a pillow; and then I attacked the great pie, breaking off a corner with my hands and cramming it in my mouth. It was still warm, savory, succulent. Next time I came through the kitchen, the pastry was whole, unbroken. The enchantment held. Was it that, as a dream, I could change nothing of this deep reality of sleep?"

So he stays there. He has always been alone, that is nothing new; and now he is not hungry. Not even sexually, for he shares a sleeping peasant girl with her sleeping lover, and she smiles with pleasure in her sleep, and there is no harm in it, for the spell holds: nothing can be changed, or broken, or hurt. What more can he desire?

Speech, perhaps, which he never had much of in his old life either. Here there is no one to answer if he speaks; but he has vast leisure, time without end, and so he teaches himself to read. He reads the princess's book of fairy tales. He knows then where he is. Perhaps he knows what more there is to desire.

He knows who the princess is. "I knew that she, she alone in all the castle, might wake at any moment. I knew that she, alone of all of them, all of us, was dreaming. I knew that if I spoke in that tower room, she would hear me: maybe not waken, but hear me in her sleep, and her dreams would change." He knows that to break the spell, all he need do is move the spindle in her hand so that its tip does not prick into her thumb. "If I did that, if I moved the spindle, a drop of red blood would well up slowly on the delicate little cushion of flesh above the joint. And her eyes would open. Her eyes would open slowly; she would look at me. And the enchantment would be broken, the dream at an end."

My story, like Sylvia Townsend Warner's poem, merely asks a question. It does not alter anything. All will go on as told. The prince will come; his kiss will wake his virgin bride. I and my poacher had no desire to change the story. We were both just glad to get into it. To be there, awake.

Thinking about it now, I believe that the tale is as impregnable and unassailable as its hedge of thorns. We can play variations round about it, imagine peasant trespassers or rapist princes, happy or unhappy endings, as we please. We can define it; we can defile it. We can retell it to improve its morality, or try to use it to deliver a "message."

When we're done, it will still be there: the place within the thorn-hedge. The silence, the sunlight, the sleepers. The place where nothing changes. Mothers and fathers will read the tale to their children, and it will have an influence upon those children.

The story is, itself, a spell. Why would we want to break it?

Endnotes

1   Bloom, *The Anxiety of Influence; a theory of poetry.*

2   Warner, *Collected Poems*, p. 249.

Re-reading Peter Rabbit

Published under the title "Imaginary Friends" in
The New Statesman, December 18, 2006

MANY of us have at least one book or tale that we read as a child and come back to now and then for the rest of our lives. A child or grandchild to be read aloud to provides a good excuse, or we may have the courage to return, quite alone, to *Peter Rabbit* for the keen pleasure of reading language in which every word is right, the syntax is a delight in itself, and the narrative pacing is miraculous. Revisiting a book loved in childhood may be principally an indulgence in nostalgia; I knew a woman who read *The Wizard of Oz* every few years because it "made her remember being a child." But returning after a decade or two or three to *The Snow Queen* or *Kim,* you may well discover a book far less simple and unambiguous than the one you remembered. That shift and deepening of meaning can be a revelation both about the book and about yourself.

It interests me that most of these "lifelong" children's books are fantasies: books in which magic works, or animals speak, or the laws of physics yield to the laws of the human psyche.

When books written for children began to become common, along about the mid-nineteenth century, fiction was dominated by the realistic novel. Romance and satire were acceptable at least in some degree to the realists, but overt fantasy was not. So for a while, exiled from the adult world, fantasy found a refuge in children's books. There it flourished so brilliantly that people began to perceive imaginative fiction as being "for children."

The modernists extended this misconception by declaring fantastic narrative to be intrinsically childish. Though we have left modernism behind us and may already be done with postmodernism, still many critics and reviewers approach fantasy determined to keep Caliban permanently confined in the cage of kiddilit. There should be a word—maturismo, like machismo?—for the anxious savagery of the intellectual who thinks his adulthood has been impugned.

To conflate fantasy with immaturity is a rather sizable error. Rational yet non-intellectual, moral yet inexplicit, symbolic rather than allegorical, fantasy is not primitive, but primary. Many of its great texts are poetry, and its prose often approaches poetry in density of implication and imagery. The fantastic, the marvelous, the impossible rode the mainstream of literature from the epics and romances of the middle ages to Ariosto and Tasso and their imitators, to Rabelais and Spenser and Shakespeare and beyond. This is not to say that everybody approved of it. Conflict with religion and with realism always loomed. In the first great European novel, Imagination and Realism meet head-on, and their contest is the very stuff and argument of the book. Don Quixote is driven mad by chivalric fantasies—but what is he without his madness?

Shakespeare may have influenced English literature toward fantasy in a rather particular way. Spenser has Continental counterparts, but *A Midsummer Night's Dream* and *The Tempest* do not. Nowhere else in Europe did folktale, legend, medieval romance, travelers' tales, and individual genius coalesce in such works of imagination as those plays. That may be one reason why the literature I am talking about is very largely an English-language phenomenon.

It begins with, say, George MacDonald's *At the Back of the North Wind* and runs on through *Alice in Wonderland* and *Through the Looking Glass, The Wind in the Willows,* the *Just So Stories* and the *Jungle Books,* the *Pooh* books, *Dr Dolittle, The Hobbit, Mistress Masham's Repose, The Once and Future King, Charlotte's Web,* to all the serious imaginative fiction that continues to be published "for children" but is often read by adults. Does any other kind of fiction cross age-lines this way?

Realism does not. Realism comes in three separate age categories, fully recognised by publishers. Didactic, explanatory, and reassuring, realistic fiction for young children hasn't much to offer people who've already learned about dump trucks, vaccinations, and why Heather has two mommies. Realistic "Young Adult" novels tend to focus tightly on situations and problems of limited interest to anyone outside that age group. And realistic fiction for adults, with its social and historical complexities and moral and aesthetic ambiguities, becomes accessible to adolescents only as and if they mature.

As for "genre" fiction—mystery, horror, romance, science fiction—none of it is for children; they begin to read it as they approach their teens, but not before. The only kind of fiction that is read with equal (if differing) pleasure at eight and at sixteen and at sixty-eight seems to be fantasy and its close relation, the animal story.

Not all fantasy, of course. Few eight-year-olds get much out of Borges, Calvino, or Garcia Marquez. As the grip of realism weakened, the fantastic element began returning into adult fiction by various routes, magical realism being one of them. Borges and Calvino followed an older tradition, that of Voltaire and Kafka, the satiric or philosophic tale or *conte*. Yet that form, when it uses fantasy, may become accessible to children, even if not intended for them. *Animal Farm* is read by kids of nine or ten, as is *Gulliver's Travels*.

Saint-Exupéry's *The Little Prince* is a lovely example of the *conte* deliberately written (and illustrated) for both the child and the adult, enigmatic yet entertaining to the child, ambiguously transparent to the adult, fully satisfying to both.

Such "duplicity" certainly helps explain the durability of the books I am talking about. Lewis Carroll wrote to and for the child, with no winks and sniggers behind her back at the grownups. He clearly took pleasure in making the story equally absorbing for Charles Dodgson, the professor of mathematics, and for any adult who was ready to appreciate his jokes, tricks, politics, and chess moves, his half-hidden intellectual game-playing. But the important thing is that the naivety of his audience did not lead him to withhold emotional investment in the story, to "write down." On the contrary, writing for a child while keeping to a strict standard of emotional honesty seems to have freed him from facetious or merely allegorical Victorian molds, to find an inexplicit but radically vivid imagery with which to explore the intersections of reality and dream. The same is true of George MacDonald, whose fantasies for children are deeper and stranger, I think, than those he wrote for adults.

It is the strict standard of emotional honesty that counts. This is where Oscar Wilde's fairy tales fail, and sometimes Hans Andersen's. They only pretend to be for children. Disguising adult self-pity in sentimental cruelty is an unfortunately effective ploy. Andersen's tales fascinated and frightened me as a child; I read them only when I already felt morbid. But the Pan chapter of *The Wind in the Willows* I loved dearly even when I only half understood it, for its emotional exaltation is genuine. And in the last of the Mowgli tales in the *Jungle Books*, though the yearning pain of final exile from the kingdom of childhood was hardly comprehensible to me, I felt it as a truth awaiting me, and wept for it. Children don't mind you talking over their heads — they're used to it, and used to figuring it out. Anything is better than being talked down to.

The *Harry Potter* phenomenon, a fantasy aimed at sub-teenagers that became a great best-seller among adults, confirmed that fantasy builds a two-way bridge across the generation gaps. Adults trying to explain their enthusiasm told me, "I haven't read anything like that since I was ten!" And I think this was simply true. Discouraged by critical prejudice, rigid segregation of books by age and genre, and unconscious maturismo, many people literally hadn't read any imaginative literature since childhood. Rapid, immense success made this book respectable, indeed obligatory, reading. So they read it, and rediscovered the pleasure of reading fantasy — which may be inferior only to the pleasure of rereading it.

The Critics, the Monsters, and the Fantasists

THERE was a while when people kept telling me, you must read this wonderful book about a school for wizards, it's so original, there's never been anything like it!

The first time this happened, I confess I thought they were telling me to read my own *A Wizard of Earthsea*, which involves a school for wizards, and has been in print since 1969. No such luck! I had to hear all about Harry, and it was hard, at first. I felt ignoble envy. But I soon felt a growing and less ignoble astonishment. Reviewers and critics were talking about Rowling's book as if it were a unique, unprecedented phenomenon.

The true phenomenon was the huge, genuine popularity the book earned before the best-seller machinery took over. It was a charmer, in the wizardly sense of the word: it cast the narrative spell. Word-of-mouth led adults to read it who had not read anything remotely like it since they were ten, if then; and finding it new to their experience, they thought it original.

But people who write about books are supposed to have some experience in reading. Those who praised *Harry Potter* for its originality were demonstrating blank ignorance of the traditions to which it belongs—not only a British subgenre, the "school story," but also a major world tradition, the literature of fantasy. How could so many reviewers and literary critics know so little about a major field of fiction, have so little background, so few standards of comparison, that they believed a book that was typical of a tradition, indeed quite conventional, even derivative, to be a unique achievement?

The modernists are largely to blame. Edmund Wilson and his generation left a tradition of criticism that is, in its way, quite a little monster. In this school for anti-wizards, no fiction is to be taken seriously except various forms of realism, labeled "serious." The rest of narrative fiction is labeled "genre" and is dismissed unread.

Following this rule, the universities taught generations of students to shun all "genres," including fantasy (unless it was written before 1900, wasn't written in English, and/or can be labeled magical realism). Students in English departments were also taught to flee most children's books, or books that appeal to both children and adults, as if they were ripe buboes. And in many universities this still holds. Academic professionalism is at stake—possibly tenure. To touch genre is to be defiled. Reviewers in the popular journals, most of whom come out of the universities, mostly still obey the rule. If the reality of what people read forces a periodical to review mysteries or science fiction, they keep the reviews separate, in purdah, under a coy title.

Nobody can rightly judge a novel without some knowledge of the standards, expectations, devices, tropes, and history of its genre (or genres, for increasingly they mix and interbreed). The knowledge and craft a writer brings to writing fantasy, the expectations and skills a reader brings to reading it, differ significantly from those they bring to realistic fiction—or to science fiction, or the thriller, or the mystery, or the western, or the romance, or the picture book, or the chapter-book for kids, or the novel for young adults.

There are of course broad standards of competence in narrative. It would be interesting to identify writers whose narrative gift transcends genre, to find out what it is that Jane Austen, Rudyard Kipling, and Patrick O'Brian have in common (arguably a great deal). But distinction is essential to criticism, and the critic should know when a standard is inappropriate to a genre.

It might be an entertaining and educative exercise in fiction courses to make students discover inappropriate standards by using them. For example: Judge *The Lord of the Rings* as if it were a late-twentieth century realistic novel. (Deficient in self-evident relevance, in sexual and erotic components, in individual psychological complexity, in explicit social references... Exercise too easy, has been done a thousand times.)

Judge *Moby Dick* as science fiction. (Strong on technological information and on motivation, and when the story moves, it moves; but crippled by the author's foot-dragging and endless self-indulgence in pompous abstractions, fancy language, and rant.)

Judge *Pride and Prejudice* as a Western. (A pretty poor show all round. Women talking. Darcy is a good man and could be a first-rate rancher, even if he does use those fool little pancake saddles, but with a first name like Fitzwilliam, he'll never make it in Wyoming.)

And to reverse the whole misbegotten procedure: Judge modern realist fiction by the standards of fantasy. (A narrow focus on daily details of contemporary human affairs; trapped in representationalism, suffocatingly unimaginative, frequently trivial, and ominously anthropocentric.)

The mandarins of modernism and some of the pundits of postmodernism were shocked to be told that a fantasy trilogy by a professor of philology is the best-loved English novel of the twentieth century. Why were they surprised?

Until the eighteenth century in Europe, imaginative fiction *was* fiction. Realism in fiction is a recent literary invention, not much older than the steam engine and probably related to it. Whence the improbable claim that it is the only form of fiction deserving to be admired and loved?

The particular way we make distinctions between factual and fictional narrative is also quite recent, and though useful, inevitably unreliable. As soon as you tell a story, it turns into fiction (or, as Borges put it, all narrative is fiction). It appears that in trying to resist this ineluctable process, or deny it, we of the Scientific West have come to place inordinate value on fiction that pretends to be, or looks awfully like, fact.

But in doing so, we've forgotten how to read the fiction that most fully exploits fictionality.

I'm not saying people don't read fantasy; a whole lot of us *people* do; but our scholars and critics for the most part don't read it and don't know how to read it. I feel shame for them. Sometimes I feel rage. I want to say to the literature teacher who remains wilfully, even boastfully ignorant of a major element of contemporary fiction: you are incompetent to teach or judge your subject. Readers and students who do know the field, meanwhile, have every right to challenge your ignorant prejudice. Rise, undergraduates of the English Departments! You have nothing to lose but your A on the midterm!

And to the reviewers, I want to say, O critic, if you should come upon a fantasy, and it should awaken an atrophied sense of wonder in you, calling with siren voice to your dear little Inner Child, and you should desire to praise its incomparable originality, it would be well to have read in the literature of fantasy, so that you can make some comparisons and bring some critical intelligence to bear. Otherwise you're going to look like a Patent Office employee rushing out into the streets of Washington crying, "A discovery, amazing, unheard of! A miraculous invention, which is a circular disc, pierced with an axle, upon which vehicles may roll with incredible ease across the earth!"

I often wish I could indicate to such people that there are pleasant and easy ways to remedy their ignorance. I would like to ask them to read *The Lord of the Rings*, because to me the book is in itself a sufficient demonstration of the value of fantasy literature. But if they don't know how to read it, it will do more harm than good. They'll come away snarling *childish, primitive, escapist, simplistic,* and other mantras of the school for anti-wizards, having learned nothing.

The author of *The Lord of the Rings* was himself a scholar, and while wearing his professorial hat he wrote essays about the kind of fiction he wrote. Anybody who wants to be able to think about fantasy literature would do well to begin with them. The best introductory guide I know to the domain of fantasy is the essay in his book *The Monsters and the Critics* called—unfortunately—"On Fairy Stories."[1] (Why Tolkien, who came to have a murderous hatred of sweet little fairies of the Tinker Bell breed, used that phrase instead of the already acceptable words *fantasy* or *fantastic* literature, I don't know; but he did. All professors have a streak of madness.) At any rate, it is perfectly possible to disagree with Tolkien's explanation and justification of the nature of fantasy, but it is really not admissible to talk seriously about fantasy without knowing what he said. Critics and academics who refuse to recognise fantasy as literature must at the very least have read Tolkien, both as critic and as novelist, and be able to justify their opinion against both his opinion and his accomplishment.

Alas, many of them read Todorov instead. Todorov said many interesting things in his book on fantasy, but few of them have anything to do with fantasy. Anyone familiar with the literature he should have read can only admire his perverse ingenuity in getting off the subject.

But then, I wonder how many of the teachers and critics who so stoutly refuse to consider fantasy as literature have read Bakhtin or Borges? Or Kroeber or Attebery, to name two of the most informed and thoughtful contemporary writers about the field?

I wonder how many of them have actually read a fantasy novel since they were nine or ten years old?

This essay designedly began by talking about a children's book, for in talking about fantasy, one can't exclude children's literature (something that evidently never occurred to Todorov).

The capacity of much fantasy literature to override age-boundaries, to me a most admirable power, is to the anti-wizards a degrading weakness. That a novel can be read by a ten-year-old implies to them that it must be faulty as an adult novel: out comes the mantra, *primitive escapist simplistic*—in a word, *childish*. "Oh, those awful orcs," Wilson squeals cutely, believing himself to be imitating a reader of fantasy. The modernists wanted so badly to be perceived as grown-ups that they left a legacy of contempt for children's literature, which is still rarely questioned. Scholars of kiddilit are relegated to a drab kindergarten annex to the canonical structure of Literature, an embarrassment to the architects of Importance.

To throw a book out of serious consideration because it was written for children, or because it is read by children, is in fact a monstrous act of anti-intellectualism. But it happens daily in academia.

The prejudice is by no means only against fantasies; any novel accessible to children is suspect. The principal reason Kipling's *Kim* has very seldom been given its rightful place in the curriculum or the canon of English novels is probably the notion that, since it can give immense delight to a twelve-year-old, it cannot possibly reward an adult reader. That this is a mistaken assumption can be proved by reading *Kim*; but prejudice is easier and safer. Respectability lies in never raising one's eyes from the texts of Flaubert or James, which can at least be guaranteed to bore most children almost as quickly as *The Swiss Family Robinson*.

Lewis Carroll is one of the few writers for children who escapes defenestration—partly, perhaps, because of his mathematical games in the Alice books, which daunt most literary people, and the hoopla about his sexuality, which allows them to speak of him, if not his texts, in adult terms, signaling and sniggering over the children's heads. So much foolishness has been written about Carroll, indeed, that I wonder if I am wise in wanting the critics and professors to talk seriously about children's books. Will they insist on burrowing after sexual perversion in the author as the only way of making the book respectable?

I have been asking for thirty years why most critics are afraid of dragons while most children, and many adults, are not. It is a question that really, by now, deserves some answer other than the repetition of mantras; for the restriction of literary fiction to a "mainstream" of realism becomes daily less tenable, more, dare I say, fantastic. It is not only the incursion from South America that must be dealt with, but the frequency of treason and defection in the ranks of contemporary literary fiction in English. What is the critic to do when he sees one of A.S. Byatt's impeccably adult, dourly sophisticated heroines turning slowly and elaborately into a troll? He (the pronoun has been considered and accepted) is being asked to deal with a fantasy: with, as Kroeber puts it, "an artistic experience of confronting as real what one knows cannot be real, the arousal of belief in the unbelievable"[2]

What does it mean, that a woman turns into a troll?

It may mean as much, and have as many meanings, as a girl's turning into Emma Bovary. It may indeed mean more, to more people. Incompleteness and suggestion are very powerful tools for the artist of our time; the impossible, the incredible, the fantastic all suggest the limitations and the falsity of ordinary perception. In the useful words quoted by Kroeber, *Madame Bovary* has "the imposing completeness of a delusion"—but we may prefer, in this age, "the broken fragment of truth."

> The untrained critic, unable to perceive
> the rules a fantasy works by, may perceive it
> as meaningless. To excuse or hide failure of
> comprehension, labels may be stuck onto
> the story—surrealist, dada, etc. But while
> surrealism is a subversion of meaning, fantasy
> is a construction of meaning, perhaps purely
> linguistic, perhaps more than that. Successful
> fantasy narrative is notable particularly for its
> strong inner coherence; its rules are not those
> of the ordinary world, but it never flouts them.
> Surrealism subverts in order to destroy, fantasy
> subverts in order to rebuild.[3]

The untrained mind trying to deal with fantasy is most likely to try to rationalise it—to "explain" it as reflecting an order outside the order of the story, whether a theological order, or psychological, or political, anything so long as it's familiar. But true fantasy is not allegory. Allegory and fantasy may overlap, as with Spenser, who obeys the rational convention of allegory yet keeps considerable freedom of invention; but Spenser is rather the exception than the model.

Rational inexplicability and avoidance of point-to-point symbolism do not automatically imply moral irresponsibility or social irrelevance. You might think critics would know that from having read the poetry of the last two hundred years; but the lesson seems not to be taken. The tendency to explain fantasy by extracting the fantastic from it and replacing it with the comprehensible reduces the radically unreal to the secondhand commonplace. Thus we have attempts to explain *The Lord of the Rings* as an apologia for Tolkien's Catholicism, or a kind of private mental asylum from his experiences in the First World War, etc. Such rationalisations may be earnestly perceived as a defense of fantasy, but are in fact refusals of it, attempts to explain it away. Only by approaching it on its own terms can a reader begin to apprehend the moral stance and the social relevance of a fantasy.

The purpose of a fantasy may be as inexplicable, in social or political terms, as the purpose (to paraphrase Maxwell) of a baby. To expect to explain or understand a fantasy as disguised ethics or politics is to fall into the reductionist trap. The purposive, utilitarian approach to fantasy and folktale of a Bettelheim or Bly, and in general the "psychological" approach to fantasy, explaining each element of the story in terms of its archetype or unconscious source or educative use, is deeply regressive; it perceives literature as magic, it is a verbomancy. To such interpreters the spell is a spell only if it works immediately to heal or reveal.

Most critics of fiction now eschew such reductive readings; even those who admit that reading a novel may have a profound and lasting effect on the mind and feelings of the reader, possibly including healing and enlightenment, are aware that the effect is not to be prescribed and often may not even be defined. If literary criticism doesn't demand purposive "meaning" of realism, why does it demand it of fantasy?

Probably because critics still equate fantasy with kiddilit. Children's books are particularly defenseless against utilitarian interpretations and judgments. I have been appalled to see my fantasies discussed in journals and columns of children's literature as if they were tracts. That there could be more to a child's book than a brisk story and an explicit ethical lesson—that children need active imagination more than closed moralities, that they respond to beauty in imagery and language, that they read to learn how to ask questions more than to be told answers—this seems to be news to those who judge children's books. But then, how much can you ask of critics and reviewers who are routinely despised and ignored by their peers and inferiors in academia and journalism?

The habit of reducing text to political-economic terms has prevented many Marxian and neo-Marxian critics from reading fantasy at all. If they can't read it as utopian, dystopian, or of clear social relevance, they're likely to dismiss it as frivolous. They see kings, and assume reactionary politics; they see wizards, and assume superstition; they see dragons, and assume nonsense. A literal mind is a great asset to reading fantasy, and so is a liberal mind, but not when either has been programmed too rigidly. Still, I welcome any socially conscious reading of fantasy, so long as it isn't ideologically puristic, for too many modern fantasies are intolerably trivial and complacent in their half-baked feudalism.

The charge that the whole enterprise of fantasy is "escapist" has been discussed by Tolkien and others, and only the ignorant continue to repeat it. It is a fact, however, that much fantasy, especially of the 'heroic' kind, seems on the face of it socially and historically regressive: withdrawing from the Industrial Revolution and Modern Times, the fantasy story is often set in a green, underpopulated world of towns and small cities surrounded by wilderness, beyond which the exact and intricate map in the frontispiece does not go. This certainly appears to be a return to the world of the folktale. So it is; and to the world of Homer, Vergil, Shakespeare, Cervantes, Swift, Wordsworth, Dickens—the world of literature and human experience until a hundred and fifty years ago or so. This world is lost now to city folk, but still inhabited by many others, and still accessible to most of us in memories of childhood, hours or days in the woods or the fields, vacations in the mountains or by the shore—the country: the world we call, since it is no longer natural to us, "nature."

Fantasy's green country is one that most of us enter with ease and pleasure, and it seems to be perfectly familiar to most children even if they've never been out of the city streets. It partakes of the Golden Age, whether mythic or personal, though it may also partake of the darkness that ends the golden ages.

Nostalgia is probably essential to it. Nostalgia is a suspect emotion these days, and I will not attempt to defend it, aside from saying that I think it fuels more great poetry, perhaps, than any other emotion. But I will defend fantasy's green country.

Tolkien's Middle Earth is not just pre-industrial. It is also pre-human and non-human. It can be seen as a late and tragic European parallel to the American myth-world where Coyote and Raven and the rest of them are getting things ready for "the people who are coming"—human beings. At the end of *The Lord of the Rings*, we know that the non-human beings of Middle Earth are "dwindling" away or passing into the West, leaving the world to mankind alone. The feeling-tone indeed is less nostalgia than bereavement, the grief of those exiled from dear community, tears by the waters of Babylon.

My Earthsea and the familiar forests and towns of much fantasy are not informed by that great vision: but I think they too imply that modern humanity is in exile, shut out from a community, an intimacy, it once knew. They do not so much lament, perhaps, as remind.

The fields and forests, the villages and byroads, once did belong to us, when we belonged to them. That is the truth of the non-industrial setting of so much fantasy. It reminds us of what we have denied, what we have exiled ourselves from.

Animals were once more to us than meat, pests, or pets: they were fellow-creatures, colleagues, dangerous equals. We might eat them; but then, they might eat us. That is at least part of the truth of my dragons. They remind us that the human is not the universal.

What fantasy often does that the realistic novel generally cannot do is include the nonhuman as essential.

The fantasy element of *Moby Dick* is Moby Dick. To include an animal as a protagonist equal with the human is — in modern terms — to write a fantasy. To include *anything* on equal footing with the human, as equal in importance, is to abandon realism.

Realistic fiction is relentlessly focused on human behavior and psychology. "The proper study of mankind is Man." When fiction disobeys Pope and begins to include the Other, it begins to shade into the ghost story, the horror story, the animal story, or science fiction, or fantasy; it begins the movement outward to the not-entirely-human.

Even "regional" fiction, always looked at disparagingly by the modernists, is part of this movement, sliding from human psychology into that which contains it, the landscape.

We need better definitions of terms than the ones we have. Hardy's Egdon Heath is in itself entirely realistic, but its centrality to *The Return of the Native* decentralises the human characters in a way quite similar to that of fantasy and even science fiction. Melville's white whale isn't a real whale, he's a beast of the imagination, like dragons or unicorns; hence *Moby Dick* is not an animal story, but it is a fantasy. Woolf's *Flush* is an animal story, because Flush is (and actually was) a real spaniel; but of course it is also a novel about the Brownings; it is also definable as a fantasy, since the dog is a central character, and we know what he is thinking; but then we know what the dog is thinking in the hunting scene in *War and Peace*, too, which does not make *War and Peace* a fantasy... The clean, sharp definition of what realism is and what fantasy is recedes ever further, along with any justification for despising genre.

I venture a non-defining statement: realistic fiction is drawn towards anthropocentrism, fantasy away from it. Although the green country of fantasy seems to be entirely the invention of human imaginations, it verges on and partakes of actual realms in which humanity is not lord and master, is not central, is not even important. In this, fantasy may come much closer to the immense overview of the exact sciences than does science fiction, which is very largely obsessed by a kind of imperialism of human knowledge and control, a colonial attitude towards the universe.

The only world we know of, now, that isn't shaped and dominated by human beings, is "long ago." "Far away" won't do any more, unless we leap to a literally other world, another planet, or into an imagined future—and these options will be labeled science fiction, even though they may well be fantasies grasping at the specious plausibility, the pseudo-rationalism, provided by popular concepts of "Science" and "the Future."

It is a fact that we as a species have lived for most of our time on earth as animals among animals, as tribes in the wilderness, as farmers, villagers, and citizens in a closely known region of farmlands and forests. Beyond the exact and intricately detailed map of local knowledge, beyond the homelands, in the blank parts of the map, lived the others, the dangerous strangers, those not in the family, those not (yet) known. Even before they learn (if they are taught) about this small world of the long human past, most children seem to feel at home in it; and many keep an affinity for it, are drawn to it. They make maps of bits of it—islands, valleys among the mountains, dream-towns with wonderful names, dream-roads that do not lead to Rome—with blank spaces all around.

The monstrous homogenization of our world has now almost destroyed the map, any map, by making every place on it exactly like every other place, and leaving no blanks. No unknown lands. A hamburger joint and a coffee shop in every block, repeated forever. No Others; nothing un-familiar. As in the Mandelbrot fractal set, the enormously large and the infinitesimally small are exactly the same, and the same leads always to the same again; there is no other; there is no escape, because there is nowhere else.

In reinventing the world of intense, unreproducible, lo-cal knowledge, seemingly by a denial or evasion of current reality, fantasists are perhaps trying to assert and explore a larger reality than we now allow ourselves. They are trying to restore the sense — to regain the knowledge — that there is somewhere else, anywhere else, where other people may live another kind of life.

The literature of imagination, even when tragic, is reassuring, not necessarily in the sense of offering nostalgic comfort, but because it offers a world large enough to contain alternatives and therefore offers hope.

The fractal world of endless repetition is appallingly fragile. There is no illusion, even, of safety in it; a human construct, it can be entirely destroyed at any moment by human agency. It is the world of the neutron bomb, the terrorist, and the next plague. It is Man studying Man alone. It is the reality trap. Is it any wonder that people want to look somewhere else? But there is no somewhere else, except in what is not human — and in our imagination.

If we want to get out of the Mandelbrot set world, that's where the roadmap is. Exact, intricate, inexplicable, and indispensable.

Endnotes

[1] Tolkien, John Ronald Reuel: *The Monsters and the Critics and Other Essays*, ed. C. Tolkien, Houghton Mifflin, 1984.

[2] Kroeber, Karl: *Romantic Fantasy and Science Fiction*, Yale, 1988, p. 48.

[3] Ibid. p. 48.

Cheek by Jowl
Animals in Children's Literature

This is a reworking and expansion of the
Arbuthnot Lecture of 2004, which I had the
pleasure of giving at a meeting of the American
Library Association. To keep the lecture from going
on all night I had to strictly limit my discussion of
the books it was about; and the talk as printed in
Children & Libraries could be only slightly longer.
In this version, I have time and room to appreciate
each book in more detail and dwell on how it
may exemplify or define or defy conventions or
traditions of the literature under discussion.

I. Human: Continuum, Dichotomy

I AM writing at a desk over which is pinned a painting from the Mexican state of Guerrero. It is in very bright colors of blue and red and orange and pink and green, and shows a village, drawn in the kind of perspective I understand — no vanishing point. There are lots of flowers the size of trees, or trees the size of flowers. This village is busy: a lady is selling pies, men are carrying sacks, a young man is proposing to a young woman, a gentleman is playing the guitar and a lady is snubbing him; people are gardening, grinding corn, cooking, coming out of church, going to school; a cowboy on a horse is herding some cows and a bull; there is a cock-fight going on; a donkey pulls a cart into town; there are rabbits, chickens, and dogs in the house yards, at least I think they're dogs although they're rather hard to tell from the goats — or are they sheep? — next door; horses carrying loads are trotting down a street past the drunk man lying on his back kicking his heels in the air; there are fish in the stream; and up on the bright green hill under the bright golden sun stand two fine stags, one bright white and one bright red.

There are almost as many animals in the painting as people, and all of them are mixed up together, cheek by jowl, except for the wild stags, who stand aloof.

If you took the animals out of the picture it wouldn't be a true picture of the village, any more than if you took the people out of it, for the villagers' lives and the animals' lives are totally entwined. Food, drink, transportation, sport: the animals provide all that to the villagers, and therefore the villagers provide for the animals; each is at the service of the other. Interdependent. A community. Cheek by jowl. And this is the way most of us have lived during the several thousand years of human history, until just the last century or two.

The two stags, the only wild animals in the picture, stand outside the village, not part of it, yet very much part of the picture.

Before history, before agriculture, we lived for hundreds of thousands of years as hunter-gatherers. A hunter-gatherer village typically consisted of people only, with maybe some pets—dogs or baby animals. Such a human community was an element in a predominately nonhuman community: forest, jungle, grassland, or desert, with its stable population of plants and animals, its ecosystem. Each species, including ours, was part of this population, this interdependent system. Each species went about its business on a more or less equal footing—the tribal village, the ant hill, the antelope herd, the wolf pack. As hunter-gatherers, our relationship to the animals was not one of using, caretaking, ownership. We were among, not above. We were a link in the food chain. We hunted deer; lions hunted us. With the animals we didn't eat and that didn't eat us, our relationship was neutral or neighborly: some neighbors are tiresome, some are useful, or liked, or laughable, or admirable.

This neighborliness or fellowship, when positive, was often seen as a spiritual kinship. In that kinship the animals were generally seen as the elders, the forerunners, the ancestors of the humans. They are the people of the Dream Time. We belonged to them, the people of the Deer or the children of the Badger. In the immense, immensely unhuman world of the stone age, the little communities of our naked, soft-skinned species, beset by both realistic and imaginary fears, needed to know and assert their fellowship, their kinship with the powerful, ancient, unchanging animal world all around it. We knew we were different, but we knew also that we belonged.

This was still knowledge to some minds as late as Lucretius, who lived just before the Christian era. In his great poem *On the Nature of Things*, Lucretius saw no barrier between man and the rest of creation; he saw the non-human world as the matrix in which mankind is formed and nourished, to which we belong as the garnet belongs to the rock in which it crystallised, and to which we will return as the sunlit wave returns into the sea.

But that is not how the tribes of the deserts of Judaea saw it. They saw the earth not as a nourishing matrix but as an antagonist, not a network of interdependence but a kingdom to be ruled. The animal was set entirely apart from both the human and the divine: and mankind was to dominate everything else by divine mandate.

The more we herded and bred animals for food and work, domesticating and dominating them, and the more we lived in cities among other humans only, the easier it was to separate ourselves from other species, to assert difference and dominance, denying kinship and its obligations. In Europe, the idea of community or neighborliness with animals became so rare that St Francis was considered strange and saintly merely for asserting it.

By the eighteenth century in Europe we'd invented "Nature." Nature comprises all the other species and all the places where they live and we don't. Idealised or demonised, Nature is humanity's Other. We stand outside it and above it.

In the forest, the village, or the farm, our interdependence with animals was unmistakable, community was a fact of life; we could despise our domestic animals, bully them, brutalise them, but we couldn't get on without them and we knew it, and so we knew them. But the cities kept growing, and the farms and the wilderness shrinking. After the Industrial Revolution, more and more people lived without any daily contact with other species. In the twentieth century, when the Ford replaced the horse, the last animal to be of essential use in cities, it became possible to live a whole life indifferent to and ignorant of other species. The animals needful to us for food and other requirements are elsewhere, in distant batteries and ranches and slaughterhouses; our dependence on them is so well hidden that we can literally not know it. It takes an informed, active, and uncomfortable imagination even to connect a living pig or hen with the plastic-wrapped slab, the batter-fried lumps. The disconnection is radical, the alienation complete. With the evidence of continuity gone, the sense of community is gone. We have made a world for ourselves alone, in which nothing matters, nothing has meaningful existence, but us. There are no Others.

In this radically impoverished, single-species world, pets have become intensely important links to the nonhuman world. Watching the many animal shows on TV gives us the illusion of being in touch with that world. Bird-watching, fishing, hunting—by now an entirely artificial hi-tech sport, but linked sentimentally to its origins: through all these we seek connection with nonhuman beings, or a reminder, however artificial, that there used to be a connection. That other people used to live here. That we had a family.

Our storytellers offer such a connection.

II. Three Literatures

On my wild and woolly ride through the millennia I pointed out three periods—tribal/prehistoric; farm, village, and city; and hi-tech industrial. Each has its literature of animals, about which I will go on generalising in the most shameless fashion.

First: The oral literatures of hunter-gatherer peoples are largely myths, in which animals are protagonists, sometimes the only protagonists.

The general purpose of a myth is to tell us who we are—who we are as a people. Mythic narrative affirms our community and our responsibilities. Myths are told as teaching-stories to both children and adults.

For example, many Native American myths concern a First People, called by animal species names such as Coyote, Raven, Rabbit, whose behavior is both human and animal; among them are creators, tricksters, heroes, and villains; what they are doing, usually, is getting the world ready for the "people who are coming," that is, us, us humans, us Yurok or Lakota. Out of context, the meaning of stories from these great mythologies may be obscure, and so they get trivialised into just-so stories—how the woodpecker got his red head, and so on. In the same way, the Jataka tales of India are retold as mere amusements, with no hint of their connection to the ideas of dharma, reincarnation, and the Buddha-nature. But a child who "gets" the story may "get" a sense of those deep connections without even knowing it.

Second: The oral and written literatures of pre-industrial civilisations are, of course, about everything under the sun, but all those I know contain a powerful and permanent element of animal story, largely in the form of folktale, fairytale, and fable, again told both to children and to adults. In these, the humans and animals mingle cheek by jowl just as in the Guerrero village.

Third: In postindustrial civilisation, where animals are held to be irrelevant to adult concerns, animal story is mostly perceived as being for children. Modern children hear or read stories from the earlier eras, both animal myths and animal fables and tales, retold and illustrated for them, because animal stories are considered suitable for children, and because children want them, seek them, demand them. There is also a modern literature of animal stories, written sometimes for children, sometimes not, but the kids usually get hold of them. Although almost all non-satirical writing about animals is automatically dismissed by literary critics as trivial, authors continue to write animal stories. They are writing in response to a real and permanent demand. Kids want animal stories. Why?

Why do most children respond both to real animals and to stories about them, fascinated by and identifying with creatures that our dominant religions and ethics consider mere objects for human use—raw material for our food, subjects of scientific experiments to benefit us, amusing curiosities of the zoo and the TV nature program, pets to improve our psychological health?

It appears that we give animal stories to children and encourage them to be interested in animals because we see children as inferior, mentally "primitive," not yet fully human: so pets and zoos and animal stories are "natural" steps on the child's way up to adult, exclusive humanity—rungs on the ladder from mindless, helpless babyhood to the full glory of intellectual maturity and mastery. Ontology recapitulating phylogeny in terms of the Great Chain of Being.

But what is it the kid is after—the baby wild with excitement at the sight of a kitten, the six-year-old spelling out *Peter Rabbit*, the twelve-year-old weeping as she reads *Black Beauty*? What is it the child perceives that her whole culture denies?

By raiding my own bookshelves, asking friends, and beseeching the patient and omniscient librarians at Multnomah County Library, I found the books to read for this essay. I hope I included all the real classics. I added some books of less literary merit as exemplary of certain types of animal story. If I knew books were read by children I included them whether or not they were published for children. I had to leave out picture books, or I'd still be reading my way through the Ark. I sadly excluded fabulous or invented animals—dragons, winged cats, etc.—a related but different subject. I had an absolutely wonderful time reading—mostly rereading—all these books, some of them after sixty years. When I tried to organise them it was less fun, and when I tried to wring a thesis or a theory out of them it wasn't much fun at all. All I can offer is a taxonomy.

The organising principle I settled on is a spectrum, running from jowl to cheek—from purely animal to purely human: from books in which animals independent of human beings are the central characters, through books where the focus is on the relationship of animal and human, to books in which animals exist principally as symbols of human qualities, behaviors, or desires.

As for the thesis, I hoped to find some answers to the question I just asked: why does the child so often, so reliably, turn for stories to the beings who do not speak? I did find some themes, some threads of guidance, but I can say now, I came out of the jungle of Critter Lit with a peacock's feather and a tiger's whisker and a white rabbit's top hat, but with no answers at all.

III. Animals Speaking: Big and Little Languages

A paradox: Nobody has ever heard an animal truly speak in human language, and yet in every literature in the world animals do speak in human language. It is so universal a convention that we hardly notice it.

> "Do you know," asked the Wart, thinking
> of the thrush, "why birds sing, or how? Is it a
> language?"
> "Of course it's a language [replies
> Archimedes, Merlyn's owl]. It isn't a big
> language like human speech, but it's large."
> "Gilbert White," said Merlyn, "remarks,
> or will remark, however you like to put it, that
> 'the language of birds is very ancient, and, like
> other ancient modes of speech, little is said, but
> much is intended....'"

> —T. H. White, *The Sword in the Stone*[1]

No other creature talks the way we do. Some birds can imitate our speech; carefully trained apes can signify wants or interests by signing words in ASL; but evidently no animal except homo sap. has the capacity, activated in infancy, that allows us to learn the full range of human language. Syntax is the key here: not just single words, but combining words, recombining. By arriving with the leash in its mouth and wagging its tail, a dog can certainly signify urgency, willingness, and walking-out-at-opposite-ends-of-leash — accurately represented in language as "It's time to go for a walk!" But I don't know how a dog can say, "She and I might have gone for a walk if it hadn't started raining so hard," and I think probably a dog can't even think it. Not all, but a lot of thought depends on language. To think about what *happened*, to imagine what *didn't* happen — to tell a story or to tell a lie — to say "the thing that is not," as the Houyhnhnms put it — you need grammar, syntax, verb tenses and modes, you need what Archimedes the owl calls "a big language."

But there's a whole lot of stuff you can say or signify without any of that wonderful equipment. Such discourse is different from ours, less than ours, a little language — but why do we refuse to call it language? Merely to ensure that we know we're superior?

As Polynesia the parrot remarks to Dr Dolittle, "Sometimes people annoy me dreadfully — such airs they put on — talking about 'the dumb animals.' Dumb! Huh!"

Some scientists use language literally as a shibboleth, to draw an uncrossable line between the human species and all other species.[2] Cartesian dualism, Christian exclusivism, and behaviorist theory all have contributed for two centuries to the doctrine that animals are machines, programmed like computers, without minds, thoughts, emotions, communicative ability, even sentience — nothing in common with human beings — despite the curious similarities of our bodies and brains and behavior.

This pseudo-scientific doctrine of absolute difference rises from and reinforces our human clannishness,
our prejudice against anybody who doesn't do things the
way we do. *Those people don't talk right, they use bad grammar, it's
all bar-bar-bar, they're barbarians, they aren't really people. They're
animals. Only we are The People: only we talk real language.* There
goes the Bandar-Log in full cry!

God in the Bible says, "Let there be light." Only we
humans, according to that bible, are in God's image. So
only God and We can say "Let there be light."

But I ask you, what is a rooster at four in the morning
saying?

Do we really have to believe that there is only one way
to talk?

I submit that most children know better. Children have
to be persuaded, convinced, that animals don't talk. They
have to be informed that there is an impassable gulf between Man and Beast, and taught not to look across it.
But so long as they disobey orders and go on looking, they
know better. They know that we and creatures physiologi-
cally like us are mutually quite comprehensible.

The reason it seems so natural for animals to talk in all
folklore and many kinds of literature is that animals do
talk, and we do understand them.

We do it by translation, mostly. So do the animals.
They don't translate our big language, or not much of it.
What the dog probably hears is "Rover, bar-bar-bar walk
blah?" but Rover was on his feet before he heard "walk,"
because he had translated our body language instantly and
accurately as "We're going walking now!" And we translate the little languages of the animals—which are mostly
"spoken" by body movements and positions and sounds

that are meaningful but are not specifically symbolic words—into our big language, with all its symbolism and syntax and subjunctives. So we understand that Rover is saying, very much like T.S. Eliot, "Hurry up, please, it's time!" And the rooster says to the darkness at four a.m., "Let there be light!" And the cat as he walks by waving his tail remarks, "I am the Cat that walks by himself, and all places are alike to me."

As this last example shows, some people are better at translating than others, and we should listen to them if we really want to know what the beasts are saying.

IV. The Animal Biography

The quality of a translation matters both literarily and ethically. A mistranslation can be a mere error, or it can be deliberate, in which case it's misrepresentation — a wrong done to the speaker. Few of the authors I'm talking about deliberately mistranslate animal behavior and communication. But some authors are particularly careful, scientifically careful, about their translations, never ascribing any feeling or intention or thought to the animal except on evidence gained by patient and methodical observation. As in all good science, the purity and austerity of the method is beautiful in itself, and if the tale is well told the result is solidly satisfying.

In the strictest form of the animal biography, the creatures do not talk or think in the "big language." The author presents the animal's perceptions and feelings within its own frame of reference, avoiding interpretation in human terms as much as possible. This "method of least interpretation" sounds cold, but it by no means excludes emotional response, and may even enhance it. It can only come from long, close, real observation of animals, which is likely to lead to identification with them. The animal biographies I selected are all particularly warm and moving books.

My prime example of scrupulous honesty is the book *Red Heifer*, by Frank Dalby Davison. It is not a book many people know of now, but the Australians quite rightly gave it their Gold Medal for Best Australian Novel in 1934. It is a fine animal story, honest and compassionate, with a fiery, fearless, and tragic heroine. It is also—and this theme will turn up again—a lament for a lost wilderness.

The most unusual thing about the heroine is that she isn't a mighty wolf or faithful dog or splendid stallion, but a cow. We don't think of cattle as heroic; only one other book on my list has a bovine protagonist, and he's a born pacifist. The red heifer is heroic: a loner, a rebel, with temperament, and considerable brains, for a cow. Range-bred, she manages to escape the round-up and return to wildness—for a while. But the range is being fenced. And so her story is the story of the growth of human power and the ruin of wilderness.

The "omniscient" narrator tells us what both humans and animals are thinking or feeling, though he does it mostly by showing what they do. What the cows do is totally cow-like; they don't talk, the description of their social interaction is accurate and truthful, and interpretation or translation of their behavior into feeling or thought is done carefully and cautiously. For example: the red cow (never named) finds her calf wandering away instead of staying with the herd. The demands of motherhood bring out her intellect,

> and at last she concluded that it was time for
> her to take him with her. This decision had
> not been quickly arrived at. She had stood
> over him for an hour or more in vacillating

doubt [. . .] She had waited, and watched
him get up and wander around [. . .] There
had been much subdued lowing and hoof-
stamping and tail-switching—indicative of a
spirit perturbed—the while she waited for the
infallible voice of instinct to speak. It spoke in
the affirmative, and so the calf was with her as
the herd grazed their way up the ridge.[3]

This is finely observed and delicately told. Understanding, sympathy, and humor should not be taken for
anthropomorphisation, which I understand rather as an
unwarranted co-optation or *colonialisation* of the animal by
the human.

Davison specifically mentions and dismisses one cher-
ished anthropomorphic myth, reinforced by many horse
stories: "She was the leader of the herd, for, in spite of romantic tale-tellers, it is the females among the wild horses
and cattle bands who provide the leaders, the males being occupied with duels among themselves and with the
propagation of the species."[4] Romance is in short supply
here. When the red heifer has won her place in the herd by
fighting another heifer, the bull comes "forward to tender
the catholic hospitality of the male." The old bull later has
to defend his place in the herd against a young bull, and
the cows' lack of interest in the long, fierce battle is gently
pragmatic: "They know that, whichever wins, there will be
one remaining."[5]

The mildness, shyness, peacefulness of the wild herd
in the wilderness has an Edenic quality; we are seeing the
Golden Age just as it disappears into the mills and slaughterhouses of human greed. How often cattle have been

used in paintings of "peace and plenty," rural serenity! But the book is ultimately a lament and a tragedy. At the end the red cow and her calf, last of the wild herd, fenced out from water, go back to their old grazing ground high in the hills, where they will die of thirst and hunger. Those final pages are full of a passionate sense of presence and absence, of yearning, of tragic loss.

Of all the books I read for this essay, perhaps *Bambi* has been most misrepresented, sentimentalised, and degraded. If when you read the title *Bambi* you visualise cute skunks with hypertrophied eyes, you are suffering from disnitis. Please, go back and read Felix Salten's book. It is a book that tries to tell what it is to be a wild deer.

The emotions of the deer are fully interpreted in human terms, but their range is plausibly limited. Forest morality consists in doing what one should according to one's kind: each being follows its own being, as leaf, squirrel, or deer, male or female. All the creatures in the novel think in words and talk to one another; interspecies conversations are frequent and charming. But Man is not in the conversation. There is no human viewpoint in the book at all.

Man is seen—by the deer—as a creature of immense, incomprehensible power, about whom they tell stories, "full of blood and suffering," in which "they were unconsciously seeking for some way to propitiate this dark power, or some way to escape it."[6] The fawn Marena has a kind of Christian vision of Man—"They say that sometime He'll come to live with us and be as gentle as we are. He'll play with us then, and the whole forest will be happy, and we'll be friends with Him." But—"Old Nettla burst out laughing. 'Let Him stay where he is and leave us in peace,' she said."[7]

The beauty of the forest is celebrated in tender descriptions of small wild lives, bird songs, leaves—two autumn leaves have a philosophical discussion of life and death—but the brutality of forest life isn't prettified. The book doesn't hide the chanciness of wild lives, the certainty of mortality, death as a fact of life. A charming squirrel's death scene is painful…but he "replaces himself" next spring. The most fearful episode in the book is a hunt; and the scene where Bambi is taken by the old stag, his mentor, to see a poacher who has been shot, is shocking and haunting.

Deer behavior is realistically presented. The fawns all play together; as they grow up they grow apart. Adult stag Bambi sees doe Faline in season, fights his young stag friends for her, and has his romance; but out of season "she no longer satisfied him completely."[8] Bambi's life is mostly solitary—"He did not much care to stay with the others." Stags are called "princes," elk stags "kings," but this is mere grandeur and majesty of language; nobody rules anybody. There is no hierarchy among the animals, there are no leaders of the herd; most of the year there is not even a herd. I am not sure which kind of deer these Austrian animals are, but the behavior Salten shows is perfectly true to the behavior of the European Red Deer as extensively studied and described by Clutton-Brock and others.

If you come to the book with memories of the Disney movie, this strict realism will surprise you. The movie, for all its brilliance and seductive power, betrays the book on every level. Where Salten works from observation of real animals, Disney uses cuteness, stereotype, and cliché. Where Salten portrays violence plainly and sternly, trying to show what the life of a wild animal is and the part human beings play in it, Disney uses fear and violence gloatingly, as dramatic ends in themselves, with no meaning beyond their immediate impact on the nerves and emotions. The awful hunt is replaced with a frightening but morally neutral forest fire. The positive ethic of the movie doesn't go beyond "animals are lovable so we (should) love them." The moral effect of the book, on the other hand, is complex and can't be stated in a few words. Rereading it at the age of seventy-three, I became aware of how its complexity had shaped and penetrated my thinking ever since I was ten or twelve. It is a beautiful book, truthful in its observations and its emotions, disturbing, austere, and subtle.

Many dog stories are animal biographies. Jack London and Albert Payson Terhune are truthful observers of dog behavior and try honestly to interpret it in its own terms, even though both have a very broad romantic streak, verging on the sentimental.

Jack London's *White Fang* is a serious and sympathetic picture of a splendid animal living a hard, chancy life, both in the wild and among men. The vigorous depiction of savage bleakness and brutality gives poignancy to the dog's eventual discovery of trust and love.

Dog behavior is accurately and knowledgeably drawn. We see the world both from human perspectives and from within White Fang's mind. His feelings and thoughts are quite within the range of ideas plausible to a dog. Like Davison and other biographers, London is careful to try to "feel out" how the animal might arrive at his judgments and not attribute improbable abstract notions to him. I am uncomfortable only with London's insistence that to White Fang all human beings are gods. Canines with a hierarchic social system offer their dominant individual pure submission; but is it worship? The spiritual implication seems to me improper, overweening. Loyal obedience to the alpha of the pack is like a soldier's loyal obedience to command; it does not immediately equate to worship of a deity, though the human alpha male may like to think so.

Salten's deer, too, regard mankind with awe; and a hound in *Bambi*, like White Fang, sees his masters as gods. But to Salten, the wild vision is truer than the tamed one. Taking Bambi to see the dead poacher, the old stag says:

> "He isn't all-powerful as they say.
> Everything that lives and grows doesn't come
> from Him. He isn't above us. He's just the same
> as we are. He has the same fears, the same
> needs, and suffers in the same way. He can be
> killed like us, and then He lies helpless on the
> ground like all the rest of us, as you see Him
> now."
>
> There was a silence.
>
> "Do you understand me, Bambi?" asked the
> old stag.
>
> "I think so," Bambi said in a whisper.
>
> "Then speak," the old stag commanded.
>
> Bambi was inspired, and said trembling,
> "There is Another who is over us all, over us
> and over Him."
>
> "Now I can go," said the old stag.[9]

London's belief that a dog considers all men to be gods inevitably suggests the equation: as dog to man, so man to god. But, he doesn't follow this logic through. Salten does.

White Fang's "outlook was bleak and materialistic. The world as he saw it was a fierce and brutal world, a world without warmth."[10] Wolf morality is kill or be killed. London relishes these stern brutalities. The dog meets real human immorality in a cruel master, the "mad god," but is rescued by the "love-master," whose patient kindness finally releases his love and melts his fierceness into touching self-surrender.

In a poorly contrived episode late in the book, White Fang kills a vengeful would-be murderer, whom the author in a fit of anthropoid grandiloquence calls "a beast—a human beast, it is true, but nevertheless so terrible a beast that he can best be characterized as carnivorous."[11] This at the end of a story portraying the nobility and dignity of a carnivorous beast! What was Jack London thinking of? The word "speciesism" is an ugly and awkward one, but it does sum up a vast history of complacency and folly.

Albert Payson Terhune's *Lad: A Dog* is a classic of dog-worship. Like many dog stories, it's a love story. Its sentimentality is innocent, and redeemed from sickliness by lots of adventure. I recall that my brother and I at thirteen and ten snickered at the ever-recurring reference to Lad's "ridiculously tiny white paws," but we devoured this and all Terhune's other books. Lad's loyalty and virtue are rather overwhelming, but then, he is a dream dog, the dog any child would dream of having; and the theme of the animal as companion, rescuer, champion—the Animal Helper—is an old and powerful one. As witness its endless exploitation in the TV series *Lassie*.

In Sheila Burnford's *The Incredible Journey*, the two dogs and a cat who are trying to get back to their people aren't helpers — on the contrary, they need and find human help along their way. Domestic animals born and bred, they move through a wilderness that isn't their world, but which they cope with pretty well — particularly the cat. They don't idolise the human family they're trying to return to, or think of them as gods; they just want to get home. And that theme of home-seeking is another old and powerful one.

Though Burnford allows some large improbabilities (the cat's ability to keep up for hundreds of miles with two fair-sized dogs is a big one), the animals are realistically perceived and described. The dogs' feelings, thoughts, and desires are thoroughly doggy. Mostly we simply see what they do. The cat's mind is largely impenetrable; he just acts — and acts just like a cat — and then washes himself. Their friendship is practical, and so is their morality: while the three are on their own in the wilderness it's kill or be killed, eat or be eaten — no euphemisms about the cat's string of murders. Burnford's realism and sober reticence give her story the credibility it needs, and a strong emotional wallop, too. Straightforward, sympathetic, gently humorous, stoically acceptant, the single-minded story of home-seeking drives straight to its irresistibly moving conclusion.

In the same way, Eric Knight's *Lassie Come-Home* avoids sentimentality and earns its affective power by showing us even more plainly the utter, unreasoning directness of the dog's motives and acts. Neither Knight's book nor Burnford's is a full "animal biography," since they recount only one episode; but in their modesty, their willingness to lay aside human understanding to try to attain an understanding of how it is for the animal, they are true to the lives they tell.

The master of the realistic animal biography is surely Ernest Thompson Seton. Whether it's a bear or a cottontail rabbit or a crow, Seton brilliantly and carefully translates animal behavior to tell us a humanly comprehensible, compassionate, moving life-story.

His intention is frankly didactic. He wants his readers to know what the "lives of the hunted" are really like, and this information has a strong moral purpose. If we know what life is like for somebody else, if we have imaginatively enjoyed and suffered with them, we will be less dismissive, less fearful or scornful of them: we will be more open to love. Our spiritual community will have been enlarged.

I chose *The Biography of a Grizzly* for this essay because it is not an "easy" book. When I was a kid I could only read it when I was feeling brave, because it made me so sad and so angry—like the old, sad, angry bear, driven out of his kingdom, a grizzly Lear.

Wahb the grizzly never speaks, though when he puts a mark on a tree it is translated: "My bath. Keep away! (Signed) WAHB"—in "a language of mud, hair, and smell, that every mountain creature could read."[12] Wahb's thoughts and reactions seem to me excellent translation of animal behavior into human language, without abstraction or self-consciousness: "Revenge is sweet, Wahb felt, though he did not exactly say it, and he went for that red-nosed bear."[13]

This is another tale of the wilderness succumbing to humans, in part—but also resisting human invasion. Men are powerful and have guns, they kill his mother and her other cubs; but Wahb kills three of them when he is adult. He has unchallenged power in his territory, partly by keeping away from human territory, except Yellowstone, where he is safe. Only old age finally defeats him.

We'll be looking at some stories in which there is a tendency to what I call moral regression, where the author uses the animal protagonists as an excuse to regress to a lower ("bestial," "inhuman") moral level — most often, to justify injustice or to wallow in violence. There is some of this regressive gloating in Jack London. There is none in Seton. He does not use the bear's brutal strength to glorify brutality, but tries to show both the splendor and the terrible sadness of the "way of the wild."

Wahb suffers much in his youth and grows up "big strong and sullen," a solitary, dangerous bear, a rogue male. The book's ethics do not privilege either strength or species: "It was all fair. The man had invaded the Bear's country, had tried to take the Bear's life, and had lost his own." Miners, who are compared to bears themselves, share Wahb's code: "Let him alone and he won't bother you," one says, and indeed the bear doesn't hurt them. He is restrained by "something that in Bear and Man is wiser than his wisdom, and that points the way at every doubtful fork in the dim and winding trail." [14]

Growing old, Wahb loses his self-assurance and lets a younger bear drive him away. He finds his way to a valley of poisonous gases which he has always avoided before. Though this may seem melodramatic or romantic, animals do sometimes choose to die, and Wahb is not shown as clearly understanding what he is doing; he is being guided again by "something wiser than his wisdom." The ending, with the Angel of the Wild Things beckoning Wahb to enter into peace and rest, quietly implies a spirituality of nature not at all dependent on human understanding.

Seton does dramatise his animal biographies; he does anthropomorphise his animal heroes, sometimes to a considerable extent; but I believe his fascination with and knowledge of and respect for the separate, mysterious being of the animal, his marvelous gift of poetic, accurate detail, and his sense of tragedy make him one of the most durably valuable writers a child could be given to read.

With Dhan Mukerji's *Gay-Neck* we move from interpretation of behavior, given in the voice of the boy who owns and trains the pigeon, to autobiographical narration by the bird himself. Early in the book there are passages like this: "Then he cooed, which meant, 'Why do you send me away?' She, the mother, just pecked him the more, meaning, 'Please go. The business on hand is very serious.'"[15] The owner/narrator legitimately translates his close observation into speech expressing emotions assumed to be shared by humans and animals. But later, our human narrator says the bird must tell his own story: "It is not hard for us to understand him if we use the grammar of fancy and the dictionary of imagination." And Gay-Neck begins, most charmingly—he is, after all, an Oriental pigeon—"O, Master of many tongues, O wizard of all languages human and animal, listen to my tale…"[16]

Certainly Gay-Neck is the best one to tell us what it was like to carry messages, on the delicate wings of a bird, over the battlefields of the First World War. The distress, fear, and above all the incomprehension of his narrative are touching and credible: how is a carrier-pigeon to understand mass violence on the human scale? The human species is perceived as owning the power in this world, but not as deserving it. Humans and animals share the world and have responsibilities towards it and towards one another.

At the end of the war, the pigeon and his human companion both come home shell-shocked, traumatized, sick from what they have seen. They find healing in a lamasery. The man learns to pray, "Lead me from the unreal to the real, from darkness into light." The bird, in his own morning worship, flies to salute the rising sun. The book is admirable in its tender but unsentimental vision of man and bird as suffering creatures, equal souls.

The founding classic of the animal autobiography, surely, is Anna Sewell's *Black Beauty*. It is of course a teaching, preaching story, meant to make us walk in horseshoes and feel what horses undergo at our hands. It is also a fine novel with vivid characters and a strong sense of friendship and of delight. It is thoroughly "Victorian" in its acceptance of social and species hierarchy, but never confuses class with virtue: Lady W. and the cab-owner Skinner are as cruel as the cab-driver Jerry and the hostler Joe are kind. Beauty himself is no rebel, but neither is he a snob. Anybody who has ever known a good horse will recognise the quality of his patience and his self-respect.

Beauty tells his story in a strong, clean, direct prose, just what a well-brought-up horse ought to speak; his vocabulary and power of comparison go far beyond anything a horse could think, of course, but his knowledge and observations are singularly convincing. Anna Sewell excels in "speaking for animals"—translating sensation and emotion into words—partly, I think, because the words are direct and yet restrained. It is curious how a story so full of pain, fear, injustice, and cruelty can leave one with such a sense of justice and even of nobility; it has a strength and dignity that no other horse story quite matches. I hope it will continue to have many tears wept on its pages. They are the best sort of tears.

Having taken so much exception to the Disney movie of *Bambi*, it is a pleasure to recommend and praise the 1994 film by Caroline Thompson of *Black Beauty*, a touching, light-handed movie, true to the book, and full of lovely, lyrical photography of horses enjoying being horses.

As an example of the continuing tradition of animal autobiography in the cautionary mode, I chose Marion Ashmore's charming dog story, *Lost, Stolen, or Strayed*, now being read by the third generation in my family (*Black Beauty* is in the fourth). Its drama and warning involve dog thieves. The convention in these autobiographies, as in many animal stories, is that the animal can tell his tale to us and understand what human beings say, but does not speak to human beings, only to other animals. Woppets the terrier strains this convention a bit, being improbably afraid of being sent to France because they don't speak English there. But in general he is simply a nice little dog, acting doggy, his psychology interpreted in human terms but with no improbable thoughts or feelings.

As an example of the continuation of the Seton tradition, the animal telling you its life-story so you know what its life is like, I chose Frank Lindermann's *Stumpy*. It is an odd book. Lindermann so faithfully limits Stumpy's voice to the forgetful, happy-go-lucky experience of a small, fast-moving prey animal, that our hero comes off a bit unsympathetic, losing a wife here, a friend there, no big deal... But then, should a chipmunk have to act out a tragedy? Life in the moment is all there is for Stumpy — curious, interested, distractable, rejecting grief, forgetting fear.

To this small, wild creature, nobody owns the world; who has the power is not really an issue, as it is in so many animal stories. Everybody, including the few humans Stumpy sees, is part of the world; no species has special status. He calls members of other species "pine-squirrel person" or "toad person," even "echo-person," the one who repeats one's call. This is a Native American usage reflecting an acceptance of a nonhierarchical view of animals as persons and persons as animals, everybody on an equal footing in a wild world.

But Stumpy can be a bit dry about us. After he and a friend see an eagle kill a coot they talk about it:

"Everybody has enemies," I told him, feeling a little sorry for the coot.

"Maybe," he said. "But tell me, who is the enemy of the eagle, Stumpy?"

"Man," I said.

"And who is man's enemy?" he asked, as though he had me cornered.

"Man," I said again. And then we both laughed.[17]

A recent, unusual, and delightful example of animal autobiography is Caroline Alexander's *Mrs. Chippy's Last Expedition*, a journal of Shackleton's third voyage to the

Antarctic, related by the ship-carpenter's cat. It is a true story, illustrated by photographs. Caroline Alexander knows everything that can be known about those men on that awful trip, and she also writes with aplomb and authenticity in the voice of a tomcat. As the cat sees it, he is in full control of the expedition from beginning to end. It is an extremely funny book, and the hero's serenity in desperate situations is very fine. If I were reading it aloud to a child, though, I might have trouble at the very end. They always say Shackleton never lost a man, but they don't talk about the animals.

V. The Animal Novel

In animal autobiographies, the animals relate their story to us, a pure literary convention. They may understand human speech or they may not, but they don't talk to or with humans, only to other animals. This same separation of human and animal communication holds in my next category of animal-centered books, which I call the animal novel.

We are still on the Jowl side of my spectrum. Animals are the protagonists. Human beings may run the world, but they are secondary characters in the story.

Though animal behavior in these books may be species-characteristic and may have a great deal of observation-based realism, they differ from the biographies in containing a fantasy element: what the animals do is a mixture of behavior proper to their species and human behavior. Black Beauty and Wahb do only what a horse or a bear would do. Animal novel heroes act from reasoned motives or for ends that (as far as we know) are human motives and aims not shared by any other species. And some of them use tools, wear clothes, drive cars, have wars—owning technologies and acting out patterns of behavior that are strictly human.

There is no explanation, no justification of this blending of animal and human in any of the books that do it. They all simply assume it will be accepted, and it is. Could there be stronger evidence of the felt community of human and animal than such an unapologetic and successful assertion of it? Beatrix Potter was a superb naturalist; her Peter Rabbit is absolutely a rabbit; but he also wears clothes and drinks tea — just as Coyote, in the legends, may carry a bow or make fire.

My first example of this mode is Rudyard Kipling's story "The White Seal." One may forget that less that half the stories in Kipling's *Jungle Books* are about Mowgli; the others are very various, though they all involve animals in one way or another. Every one of them would be well worth discussing; indeed, Kipling, so often dismissed as a blustering imperialist boasting of the White Man's burden, deserves to be recognised as a singularly sympathetic and subtle writer about animals, women, children, and other inferior beings. It was hard to bypass "Rikki-Tikki-Tavi" and several others, but I couldn't talk about all the stories, and so chose "The White Seal."

It begins like a biography, with grand realistic descriptions of a fur seal growing up, and seal colonies, and mating battles; but then it takes off in a new direction, when Kotik realises — as no seal could in fact realise — that his people are objects of genocide, and that he is called to seek a haven for them where men cannot find and kill them. His odyssey in finding that place makes a great wish-fulfillment story, full of poetry and adventure, that has grown less plausible but even more poignant in the hundred and ten years since it was written.

Two modern classics of the animal novel are E.B. White's *Charlotte's Web* and Robert C. O'Brien's *Mrs Frisby and the Rats of Nimh*. In both, the animals think and speak like human beings and act out dramas that are a mixture of animal and human problems and solutions.

Charlotte's Web begins with a human point of view, the child Fern, but the point of view shifts quite soon to the animals. They talk, they act; Fern listens. She understands animal language, though she never speaks it. And here we strike a theme that runs deep in animal stories: the child is in touch with animals, but only while she is a child. Only the virgin can touch the unicorn. As Mowgli comes into his manhood, he must leave the jungle. Once Henry Fussy becomes important to Fern, she doesn't listen to the animals any more — she can't hear them.

One reason kids like E.B. White's book, I think, is that it's about justice and injustice. Is it fair for a farmer to kill a runt pig? Has a spider a right to kill flies? These questions are discussed openly and firmly. And it is a mutual aid story, beast helping beast, a fine variation on the folktale theme of the Animal Helper. And finally it is a tale of the golden age, the peaceable kingdom, the old rural American dream, the farm children dream of, the farm we wish they could live on…

Mrs Frisby and the Rats of Nimh is totally animal-centered; there are no human characters; but though humans are offstage, they are powerful and dangerous—they control the world. The scientists of NIMH have altered the rats' very nature, enhancing their longevity and intelligence.

The only tame animal in the story, the farm cat, appears as an enemy: it's on the human side, not the animal side. Yet it never speaks, and it acts just like a cat, while the so-called "wild" mice wear clothes, use furniture, have both speech and reason. There are other anomalies of this kind. The rats' intelligence has been artificially enhanced in the laboratory, while the mouse Mrs Frisby hasn't been "enhanced" like the rats, yet she seems quite as intelligent as they; her "enhanced" husband even taught her to read, though not as well as her children can. There is a certain incoherence here.

Some people are impatient with such quibbles with fantasy—"Well, none of it's real, what does it matter that it's inconsistent?" It matters. The farther a story departs from accepted reality, the more it relies on its own inner consistency. By giving us a "scientific" explanation of why the rats act like humans but no explanation of why the mice also act like humans, O'Brien puts our willing suspension of disbelief into a quandary. That most of us read the book at least the first time without thinking about the inconsistency shows, perhaps, how willing we are to believe and accept our fellow-feeling with these morally troubled creatures.

For *Mrs Frisby* , too, is about justice. First, the unstated but fundamental question of the right of human beings to imprison and experiment on animals: the rats and mice don't discuss this, but in escaping from the laboratory they clearly state their right to life, liberty, and the pursuit of happiness. Then comes the poignant question, "Where does a group of civilized rats fit in?" They used to live by stealing from humans, but now, as creatures with human intelligence, they see such dependence as ethically wrong, degrading. They must create an independent, new civilization of their own. The unnaturalness of their situation, the risks they run, the fragility of their utopian vision, are vividly described.

The book is again a tale of mutual aid among animals. The sense of the need to collaborate, even to the point of self-sacrifice, is strong. But humans are excluded from the collaboration; they are the enemy, they are what the animals have to help each other against. And though the book has a satisfyingly happy finale, I'm not sure that I have much confidence that the rats' utopia in the hidden valley can endure. There's an awful lot stacked against them. That unstated darkness makes the book all the deeper in the end.

In Brian Jacques' *Redwall* there are no human characters at all. The chief protagonists are mice. A few words, such as "paw" for hand, are used to remind us that the mice have animal bodies, but since they wear clothes, farm with tools, live in a great abbey building, write books, and so on, it is hard to keep their animal bodies in view. These are civilised creatures, leading a human not an animal existence. Readers with literal minds and a craving for consistency may be worried by some aspects of this arrangement. For example, the mice of Redwall Abbey drink goat's milk and make goat's milk cheese, but there seem to be no goats at the Abbey; and even if there were, I for one would like to be told explicitly just how a mouse could milk a goat.

A reader might have a more general question: why are they called mice when they don't do anything mice do, but act just like a lot of bloody-minded feudal humans? The popularity of the Redwall books shows that this question is overly rational. Given the mouse stereotype of small-harmless-cute, simply the fact of calling them mice evidently makes them less daunting to a child reader than bloody-minded feudal humans. And *Redwall* is a fantasy. Brian Jacques makes no pretense of realism. I'm willing to say that my inability to believe his mice are mice is my own problem.

My ethical problem with the book is perhaps more legitimate. In *Redwall*, goodness and badness, admirable and base behavior, are species-specific. Mice are good, rats are bad. A badger, hedgehogs, squirrels, otters, moles, and a hare are on the mouse side — all good; weasels, stoats, and ferrets are on the rats' side — all despicable. A poison adder is, predictably, evil. A few animals are more complex: foxes play both ends against the middle, shrews are independent, an owl threatening but foolish. It's surprising to find a cat helping the hero mouse, but then, he's an aristocratic cat, and the mice are all aristocrats — "gennelbeasts." For the rigid moral hierarchy by species is also a social hierarchy: rats are rabble, moles and such are other common folk who "tug their snouts respectfully" when addressing the noble mice. The good mice and the good badger speak standard English and can read and write; moles and other good but low-class types speak dialect.

The most villainous of the rats organises an army, and the mice, though natively peaceable, go to war and defeat this threat to their feudal wellbeing. This is a plot that may well strike a reader of *The Wind in the Willows* as familiar. Indeed, some of the implausibilities concerning size and mechanical ability may seem familiar for the same reason. But *Redwall* was written in 1996, not 1908. Kenneth Grahame lived within the kind of settled hierarchical society, such a favorable environment for the upper classes, so kind and safe for them if for no one else, that Jacques nostalgically evokes. It would be historically unrealistic to ask of Grahame the perspective on the justice of that society that one can fairly ask of any late-twentieth century writer. To offer children a vision of a kind, safe world is a good thing to do; they need such visions. But I'd like the book better if a child reading it found any acknowledgment that status isn't virtue and that being born an upperclass mouse or a low-class rat is undeserved, blind, good or bad luck. I have to admit that all the way through, I was rooting for the rats. But I read the book first as an adult; as a child I'd probably have happily accepted the injustice in order to get the reassurance.

I have a similar but more serious issue with Richard Adams' *Watership Down*. Rabbits are the protagonists of this strong, well-written novel. Power in the rabbits' world belongs above all to humans and their terrible machines and weapons. Weasels, dogs, and foxes are dangers, not superior beings; the rabbits count on escaping and outwitting such enemies; and perhaps even the humans may be outwitted and evaded. This seems perfectly realistic, sound rabbit psychology and sets the scene for a drama of tragedy and hope. The rabbits speak "Lapine" and can communicate with other animals; they have poetry and a kind of religion, but they don't wear clothes, build houses, etc. — they are wild rabbits, living like wild rabbits. Or are they?

The author cites R.M. Lockley's authoritative observational study *The Private Life of the Rabbit* several times and is insistent upon Lockley as the source of some of the more extraordinary facts of the story (such as reabsorption of fetuses by stressed doe rabbits). He departs radically from Lockley and actual rabbit social behavior, however, in giving the warrens an aggressive hierarchic structure with one Chief Rabbit and a militaristic band of henchmen or soldiers, the Owsla—all male. Doe rabbits, in the book, are mindless breeding slaves. Their only function is to dig holes, provide sex, bear litters, and raise the kittens. The buck rabbits do all the thinking, planning, and acting and are in unquestioned control of the females at all times. The does are so far beneath notice, in fact, that a band of bucks fleeing the home warren to establish a new one doesn't even think to bring any does along; the guys go on for two hundred pages before it dawns on them that it may be hard to establish a new warren without females. So, in good militaristic fashion, they go and rape the Sabines: they carry off females from another warren. That the females might have any voice in the matter is not even considered.

The existence of a "Chief Rabbit" would be authorised by Lockley's term "king" for the dominant male of a group, if Adams did not ignore his equivalent term for the dominant female, the "queen." (The king rabbit wins the most battles and has access to the most females—but not free access: the queen chooses her mate and her dwelling place.) Adams shows wild rabbit society as a militaristic male hierarchy, in the teeth of Lockley's unequivocal statement that "The doe is the centre of the rabbit community, a matriarchy," and his descriptions of a wild rabbit warren as an "expanded population scattered around the queen or matriarch at the heart of the community."

It is quite extraordinary to cite a book as the source of one's information and then systematically misrepresent that information. Adams' excuse might be that Lockley himself, while stating clearly that the female is the center of rabbit society and the founder of both warren and family, prefers to talk about male behavior, which is far more easily observable, and spends much of the book describing individual males. And Lockley makes sweeping generalisations, explicitly including humans, to the effect that all females always want to stay home and tend babies—despite his own statement: "It is always the doe who initiates the new colony."

So some of Adams' sexism is ascribable to Lockley. But the militarism that Adams represents as true to wild rabbit behavior is completely his own invention. When the hero band meets their enemy, the Efrafans, the latter are evidently meant to be a perversion of wild freedom along human lines—but in fact Efrafa is merely an intensification of the oppressive regime of the other warrens. Seeing only active adult males as worthy of interest, the author presents the very limited liberality of Hazel's band as perfect democracy, righteously opposed to the Nazi rigidity of Efrafa. I see both as unrighteous, unrabbitlike, and inhuman.

> The kind of ideas that have become natural to many male human beings in thinking of females—ideas of protection, fidelity, romantic love and so on—are, of course, unknown to rabbits, although rabbits certainly do form exclusive attachments much more frequently than most people realise. However, they are not romantic and it came naturally to Hazel and Holly to consider the two Nuthanger does simply as breeding stock for the warren. This was what they had risked their lives for.[18]

In this passage the author offers a false alternative: a "romantic" ideal of the male protecting and lovingly faithful to the female, or a "natural" use by males of females as owned objects, breeding stock — thus justifying rape. No other possibility is imagined, such as a relationship of equality, or a relationship that the female initiates or controls some aspects of. Yet to read Lockley is to learn that doe rabbits take the more active and responsible role in *all* situations except male battles for dominance, and that dominant doe rabbits accept or reject male suitors as they please.

I might try to swallow the egregious sexism of the book in order to appreciate its virtues; but I won't, because Adams cheated. He wanted to write a fantasy of male superiority — all right, some people like that sort of thing. But he misrepresented Lockley's actual description of rabbit behaviors. That is cheating. It was clever cheating, too, because in 1972 blatant male supremacism was becoming less acceptable, and Adams got away with it by passing it off as animal behavior. People could say, "Oh well, it's just rabbits, after all." Only it isn't rabbits at all. Rabbits do not behave that way. A book that falsifies animal behavior as a mask for the indulgence of fantasies of morally regressive human behavior is not, to my mind, a book to give any child, or any adult either.

A recent novel, *Fire Bringer*, by David Clement-Davies, has some troubling similarities to *Watership Down*. Like Adams, Clement-Davies had unusually careful scientific observation in highly readable form to rely on: F.F. Darling's and T.H. Clutton-Brock's famous studies of Scottish red deer society. These authoritative studies show that the "harems" controlled by stags are a brief, unstable phenomenon of rutting season; for eleven months of the year stags and hinds don't mingle at all. The only lasting associations between individuals are hinds and their dependent fawns; and the groups, male or female, have no leaders. But Clement-Davies simply flouts their careful descriptions of gender relations; he shows stags leading and dominating females all year long and maintaining a rigid militaristic hierarchy, which degenerates, under a megalomaniac leader, into a cruel, coercive social order along fascist lines, like Adams' Efrafa.

The intrigues and plots and war-making, the deliberate cruelty and torture, the massiveness of the final battle—"The whole plain became a mass of fighting deer"—in all this there is a fundamental disrespect for the very nature, the *deerness* of deer—a wilful wrongheadedness. It is a pity, because there are elements in the book of an interesting vision of a religion common to human and animal: Herne, who to the deer is the Lord of the Deer, to the Scottish crofters is Herne the Hunter, the Horned Man—the man-beast figure that goes right back to Old Stone Age cave paintings. But the development of these ideas is confused and strained. A book that brought out a spiritual element in deer existence, while respecting and staying true to the reality of deer gender and society, would be more satisfying. Of course, we have a book that does just that, and I am happy to name it again: it's called *Bambi*.

As I have suggested, Kenneth Grahame may well be the unwitting founder of the lineage of several of the books I've talked about. In *The Wind in the Willows*, as in *Redwall*, virtue is a matter of species: weasels, stoats, ferrets are all bad by nature, villainously vulgar. The book reflects the ruthlessly classed society of England of 1908, along with the widespread human negativity towards certain species. Even given the benefit of historical relativism, this moral genotyping can make the reader a bit queasy. Grahame does assign a fortune and a fine estate to a toad; but Toad is not a noble soul... He is, however, a great character. This modest, funny, sunny book for children rises above the limitations of the society it was written in and for, into the universality of literature.

The Wind in the Willows takes huge risks. *Redwall's* human-acting mice may seem more plausible because there aren't any people in their world. Grahame's animals dress like people, talk like people, go mad over motor cars like peo ple—and yet there are human beings in the story right along with them. And—here's where the fantasy is won-derfully audacious—the human beings are in the animals' world, not the other way round. When Toad is jailed as a car-thief, the jailer's daughter helps him escape, disguised as her aunt the washerwoman. Shepard's illustration of this is marvelous—is the aunt toad-size or is the toad aunt-size? It does not matter. We are in a world where the human and the animal interact as equals—the world of myth and folktale, miraculously recaptured in this sunlit, nostalgic romance.

It's no accident that the god we meet here is Pan. Like Herne, Pan is very, very old: both man and beast, both for-est creature and herdsman, he gives his name to the blind terror of the wild places, yet he cares for the little ones who wander off and are lost. I don't know whether the Pan chapter of *The Wind in the Willows* or the chapter where Mole finds his old home is the more beautiful, but I know that both of them can strike deep chords of feeling, thrilling literary revelations to a child, permanent treasures to an adult.

VI. Jowl Meets Cheek

Now I come to the kind of book that might be seen as the typical animal story—tales of the relationship between human and animal. A boy and a dog. A girl and a horse.

Many of the books I call animal biographies could be put under this heading too: White Fang, Gay-Neck, Lad, Black Beauty, all have strong emotional bonds with their human owners or others. And in almost all the animal biographies and novels, the world animals live in is controlled by or tremendously influenced by human beings. But still, in those books the animal is at the center of the story.

With Will James's *Smoky* we're at a crossover point— *Smoky* is a fine biography of a horse, but it's also a fine portrait of a cowboy, and of the relationship of the cowboy and the horse, and of life on the range. Smoky and his cowboy Clint are at the same time stereotypes and vivid individuals—as the characters in a good Western generally are.

Smoky thinks and "figgers" a good deal, but all in horse terms; the conflation of thought and feeling is strong, easy, and convincing. The book gives a fascinating, knowledgeable picture of the work cowponies and their riders did (and still do), as well as being a morality tale, like *Black Beauty*, about how horses are treated, the good and the bad they meet with at the hands of men. Unfortunately James was less fair-minded toward men than toward horses: the men who mistreat Smoky are mostly Mexicans or "breeds." It's a shame that racial prejudice stains what is otherwise essentially a story about love and trust, and a lovable story.

In these books the central human-animal relationship is positive, involving the growth of trust, dependence, companionship. In some of them it is enabling, liberating, even redemptive—to the animal, the human, or both. But there may be negative connections too, involving the wild animal's only too realistic fear of the human, as in *Bambi* and many Seton stories, or the human abuse of tamed animals, as in episodes in *Black Beauty*, *White Fang*, and *Smoky*.

Straightforward classics of the positive, loving, enabling relationship between child and animal are Walter Farley's *The Black Stallion* and Marguerite Henry's *Misty of Chincoteague*—and all the galloping herd of their descendants by many other authors.

The Black Stallion generally behaves like a horse, but is super-large, super-fast, super-dangerous—a superhorse, embodying a boy's dreams of power, glory, freedom, victory. The heart of the story consists in the growth of trust and loyalty between the boy and the horse. The fascination of the stallion is in his wildness, but that beauty and natural freedom of the animal must be tamed to the purposes of mankind—"conquered."

The stallion is repeatedly described as a killer: "Here was the wildest of all wild animals—he had fought for everything he had ever needed, for food, for leadership, for life itself; it was his nature to kill or be killed."[19] In fact, the only thing wild stallions fight for is ownership of mares, here apparently considered as "leadership." Horses are prey animals. They don't fight one another for their grass or fodder. The competitive streak innate in many horses and bred for in Thoroughbreds is here weirdly exaggerated into a sort of Attila the Hun mentality.

The Black is "conquered with kindness," not with brutality. The growing relationship between boy and horse cast away on a desert island is romantic but not impossible; the scenes of training the horse to the saddle and bridle are accurate. But the race that climaxes the story is just dream stuff. Farley, who grew up with horses and horsemen, certainly knew how stupid it would be to enter an evil-tempered and headstrong stallion that had never run a race, ridden by a boy who had never ridden a race, against two experienced race horses and their jockeys. Still, one can imagine that if The Black had lost the race, Alec would have loved him almost as much as before. The stallion is in his way the Animal Helper, won by kindness, helping the boy become a manly man.

Wildness is also a theme in *Misty of Chincoteague*, but it's not equated with violent aggression, nor are taming and training glorified as conquest. The children long to capture, ride, and own the semi-feral ponies, but they learn that the only way they can do it is through kindness, patience, steadiness, courage. Their devotion to the ponies brings out the best in them—again, a gift of the beast.

And the final climax of the story glorifies freedom. The Phantom's colt stays to be tamed by the children, but the mare herself belongs to the "isle of the wild things," and the moment of her liberation is a lovely one. *Misty*, like the *Black Stallion*, is a dream story for the horse-loving child, but it's a little closer to the complicated reality a horse-loving child discovers if she actually gets to be around horses.

Enid Bagnold's *National Velvet* was not written for children, but as a delicately satirical comedy of human relationships and ambitions. Horse-loving children got hold of it right away and never let go. And quite right too, for it is a fully sympathetic picture of the particularly intense passion girls may have for horses. The four girls, their mother, and the trainer are the central characters, and the animals are mostly seen through their eyes (the only anthropomorphic moment is a fine comic one, when a terrier answers an inquiry about his love life — "Succulent," he replies succinctly.) The piebald horse is not as romantically glamorous as the Black Stallion, but he is a wonderfully vivid creature; and his training to run in the Grand National and Velvet's training to ride as his jockey are far more plausible and interesting than the race preparations in *The Black Stallion*. The fairytale element is that Velvet does ride the Pie to victory: but it's a victory one can believe—half earned, half luck—and declared invalid by the judges... The book has no simple moral message; but the author's loathing of media publicity as shameless, soulless exploitation (a large part of what the story is really about) and her admiration for courage, modesty, steadfastness, and devotion, leave a child, or any reader, on solid ground.

With Walt Morey's *Gentle Ben*, where boy saves bear and bear saves boy, we enter fully the theme of mutual aid, the realm of the Animal Helper. Fred Gypson's *Old Yeller*, where dog rescues boy but boy in the end can't rescue dog, is a fine, sad variation on the theme.

Jean Craighead George's novel *Julie of the Wolves* is a notably successful mixture of several themes and subjects. Her tale of a girl surviving in the wilderness by imitating and to some extent befriending wolves has elements in it of the Animal Helper and the lament for the vanishing wilderness, along with a good deal of both wilderness lore and Native American lore and attitudes.

At the beginning of the story we're in a world where human beings are not all-powerful—anything but. The girl Miyax, lost in the wilderness, is quite literally living a Stone Age existence, where being human does not give her an advantage over everybody else. Among the wolves, she is a weakling, a tolerated beggar and hanger-on, who has to be very careful of her manners just to stay alive. Instead of humans taming an animal, animals "wild" a human. This stunning reversal is the heart of the book's fascination.

Miyax gives the wolves names, but that means nothing to them; their behavior is that of wolves, their social institutions and manners are those of wolves. That they partially include the girl in their tribe or family is attested wolf behavior, and the author's knowledgeable description of it is wonderful. The wolves are Animal Helpers in an unusually literal and realistic sense. They tolerate, semi-adopt, and befriend Miyax. The alpha male leaves her a fresh-killed caribou as a gift. She cannot reciprocate,

she just thanks and praises. She makes a song of gratitude
for the caribou meat:

> "Amaroq, wolf, my friend,
> You are my adopted father.
> My feet shall run because of you
> My heart shall beat because of you.
> And I shall love because of you."[20]

Her sense of spiritual kinship with the wolves extends
deeply to the whole natural world. "Impulsively, she paid
tribute to the spirit of the caribou by lifting her arms to
the sun. Then, scoffing at herself for being such an old-
fashioned Eskimo, she sharpened her man's knife on a
stone and set to work."[21]

In the wilderness, among the wolves, physical superiority is pretty much moral superiority, where might makes
right: but, with one mean-natured exception to prove the
rule, the wolves are generous and affectionate, and Amaroq, the pack leader, embodies a wild nobility.

In contrast, when Miyax makes her way back to her
own kind at last, she finds human morality hideously de-
fective. The father she has longed for and looks up to is
the man who shot Amaroq from a plane, laughing, for
no reason but to kill. In the larger world she enters at the
end of the book, it is the humans who have power, and
the wolves and wilderness are doomed. "The hour of the
wolf and the Eskimo is over."

The deeply pessimistic ending doesn't entirely fit the
story of a thirteen-year-old girl so completely competent
in all the ways of survival, so ready to cope with or escape from anything including the feebleminded husband

foisted on her, and with such an irrepressibly hopeful and serene spirit. The wilderness is passing and the Inuit are changing, but to say their hour is over comes a little too close to the bad habit of proclaiming that alas! all the Indians are gone! I believe white folks should leave it up to the Inuit and the Indians to decide whether they're gone, and when and where they're going.

The stories of animal-human friendship I've been discussing, all more or less realistic, have a fantasy counterpart for younger children. Some of our animal friends are stuffed. One of them is covered with velveteen. The most famous of them are Pooh and Piglet and that lot. I won't dwell on their part in literature, because I'm only talking about flesh-and-blood animals. But as one who lived for years with stuffed animals, dear friends and active companions, far more autonomous, adventurous, and unpredictable than any doll I ever met, I wanted to mention them, and to suggest that, along the borders of reality and imagination, the human and the animal may truly participate in each other's being. Now I must go back to the unstuffed animals.

Three great works of children's literature and animal literature are *Dr Dolittle*, *The Jungle Books*, and *The Sword in the Stone*. They are all about the relationship of human and animal. In each it is different, and each explores it in depth.

Such language may sound a bit fancy, talking of *Dr Dolittle*, but Hugh Lofting's unpretentious fantasy deserves its classic status. As in *The Wind in the Willows*, animals and people interact without the slightest plausibility and without the slightest hesitation. This is because the animals act like people, mostly. But they act better than most people. None of them does anything cruel or immoral. Gub-Gub is very piggy, to be sure, and the Lion has to be scolded by his wife before he'll help the other animals, but this is the Peaceable Kingdom, where the lion will truly lie down with the lamb. Dr Dolittle helps animals by sheltering and healing them; they begin to help him in return; and that is the theme and the basis of almost everything in the story. "So long as the birds and the beasts and the fishes are my friends, I do not have to be afraid…"[22] Every people in the world understood this theme of mutual aid, of the Animal Helper, until we drove the animals out of our streets and skyscrapers. I think every child in the world still understands it. To be friends with the animals is to be a friend and a child of the world, connected to it, nourished by it, belonging to it.

Lofting's morality is entirely sweet and sunny. In Kipling's Mowgli stories, the connections between human and animal are complex and ultimately tragic. Mowgli is a link between his village people and the people of the jungle, and like all go-betweens, all liminal figures, he is torn between the two sides, torn apart. There is no common ground between the village and the jungle; they have turned their back on each other. In every language of the animals Mowgli can say "We be of one blood, ye and I!"—but can he truly say it in Hindi? And yet that is his mother's tongue, his mother's blood. Whom must he betray?

The wolf child, the wild child, both in rare and painful reality and in Kipling's dream-story, can never, in the end, be at home. The ache of exile from Eden is there even in the first story, "Mowgli's Brothers," ever stronger in "Letting in the Jungle" and "The Spring Running." Those are heartbreaking stories. Yet from the *Jungle Books* we may also carry with us all our lives the blessing of those lazy hours and breathless adventures when boy and wolf, bear, black panther, python, speak and think and act in joyous community: the mystery and beauty of belonging, totally belonging to the wildness of the world.

I want to pay a little further tribute here to Rudyard Kipling, a most uneven genius, one of the most troubling writers of his time, and one of the most badly served by his literary judges. In his book on Kipling, Angus Wilson dismisses the *Jungle Books* in a couple of sentences as silly schoolboy stuff and doesn't deign to mention the *Just So Stories* at all. For the modernist realist, the mere presence of animals as conscious, thinking beings suffices to throw a book out of consideration as literature, while a book for young children is automatically beneath notice. Such critical prejudice, added to Kipling's own self-destructive wrong-headedness and political unpredictability, has been nearly enough to destroy his reputation as a writer. Many people are, I think, ashamed to admit that they like or admire any of his books. Even *Kim*, one of the most beautiful and original novels ever written, is seldom taught in literature courses or mentioned in the canonical lists—tainted, apparently, partly by the fact that it is accessible to children over eleven or twelve. All I can do here is offer a personal tribute: in my life, the *Just So Stories*, along with the Mother Goose rhymes, were the foundation of all poetry and story; and the *Jungle Books* have been for over sixty-five years a perennial, inexhaustible source of joy and discovery.

T.H. White's *The Sword in the Stone* is as full of animals as my Guerrero painting. In the first chapter King Arthur-to-be, currently known as the Wart, takes out a goshawk, loses him, and meets Merlyn's owl Archimedes:

> "Oh, what a lovely owl!" cried the Wart.
>
> But when he went up to it and held out his hand, the owl grew half as tall again, stood up as stiff as a poker, closed its eyes so that there was only the smallest slit to peep through [. . .] and said in a doubtful voice:
>
> "There is no owl."
>
> Then it shut its eyes entirely and looked the other way.
>
> "It's only a boy," said Merlyn.
>
> "There is no boy," said the owl hopefully, without turning round.[23]

Merlyn undertakes Arthur's education, which consists mostly of being turned into animals. Here for the first time we meet the great mythic theme of Transformation, which is a central act of shamanism, though Merlyn doesn't make any fuss about it. The boy becomes a fish, a hawk, a snake, an owl, and a badger. He participates, at thirty years per minute, in the sentience of trees, and then, at two million years per second, in the sentience of stones. All these scenes of participation in animal being are funny, vivid, startling, and wise. (The reason I cite *The Sword in the Stone* rather than *The Once and Future King* is that when incorporating the first book into the trilogy, White revised out some of the finest passages, replacing the snake with a trite political satire about ants, and the cosmic vision with a visit to the wild geese—a nice chapter, but a heavy loss.)

When a witch puts Wart into a cage to fatten him up, the goat in the next cage plays Animal Helper and rescues them all. All animals rightly trust Wart, which is proof of his true kingship. That he goes along on a boar hunt does not vitiate this trust: to White, true hunting is a genuine relationship between hunter and hunted, with implacable moral rules, and a high degree of honor and respect for the prey. The emotions aroused by hunting are powerful, and White draws them all together in the scene of the death of the hound Beaumont, killed by the boar, a passage I have never yet read without crying.

At the climax of the book, Wart can't draw the sword of kingship from the stone anvil by himself. He calls to Merlyn for help, and the animals come.

> There were otters and nightingales and
> vulgar crows and hares, and serpents and
> falcons and fishes and goats and dogs and
> dainty unicorns and newts and solitary wasps
> and goat-moth caterpillars and corkindrills
> and volcanoes and mighty trees and patient
> stones…. all, down to the smallest shrew
> mouse, had come to help on account of love.
> Wart felt his power grow.[24]

Each creature calls its special wisdom to the boy who has been one of them, one with them. The pike says, "Put your back into it," a stone says, "Cohere," a snake says, "Fold your powers together with the spirit of your mind"—and: "The Wart walked up to the great sword for the third time. He put out his right hand softly and drew it out as gently as from a scabbard."[25]

T.H. White was a man to whom animals were very important, perhaps in part because his human relationships were so tormented. But his sense of connection with non-human lives goes far beyond mere compensation; it is a passionate vision of a moral universe, a world of terrible pain and cruelty from which trust and love spring like the autumn crocus, vulnerable and unconquerable. *The Sword in the Stone*, which I first read at thirteen or so, influenced my mind and heart in ways that must be quite clear through the course of this essay, convincing me that trust cannot be limited to mankind, that love cannot be specified. It's all or nothing at all. If, called to reign, you distrust and scorn your subjects, your only kingdom will be that of greed and hate. Love and trust and be a king, and your kingdom will be the whole world. And to your coronation, among all the wondrous gifts, an "anonymous hedgehog will send four or five dirty leaves with some fleas on them."[26]

VII. Fables and Psychic Fragments

Now we've come to the purely human end of my spectrum, where the animal exists mixed with or as a reflection of the human.

In the old-fashioned fable, animals represent their species but are scarcely individuals, and their behavior is not observed but stereotyped, archetypal: the wily fox, the timid mouse. In Aesop's fables, the Jataka tales, and my example, the Grimms' *Household Tales,* animals often symbolise and enact human behaviors and qualities.

The Grimms' tales are a verbal equivalent of the painting of the Guerrero village. Of the fifty stories in my Lucy Crane translation, twenty-nine have domestic or wild animals as central or active characters, and in almost every story domestic animals are part of daily life—horses, donkeys, oxen, cattle, dogs, cats, geese. Humanity is the model of behavior and society, but humans and animals are all people on a more or less equal and individual footing. Animals and humans keep house or travel together, fool or cheat one another, cheek by jowl. This is the old world, which doesn't belong to humans, as our world does. Nobody here is boss.

In general, everybody can talk to everybody else. You can get into an argument with a bean or a sausage. All animal protagonists speak to other animals, and most speak to and are understood by human characters. In most stories where animals play a significant role, they and the humans talk together; animals speaking and behaving rationally are taken for granted. In a few stories animal speech is seen as somewhat miraculous: Falada the horse, whose capacity for speech is specifically mentioned, the talking fish in "The Fisherman and his Wife" and the birds in "The Almond Tree" and "Aschenputtel," all have some element of the supernatural. And in the rather mystical tale of "The White Snake" we meet the widespread theme of the Language of the Animals: a taste of the white snake that the king keeps in a covered dish gives the servant who tastes it the ability to understand what the animals say to one another, from which he gets power and benefit.

Religion as such plays no part in the stories (as selected and translated in this collection). Moral superiority isn't a matter of species, but is individual and unpredictable. As a rule the clever weak defeat the stupid strong, and the compassionate are helped by those they have helped. But justice in folktales is unpredictable and arbitrary; the human hero of "The White Snake" saves the lives of three starving baby ravens by killing his horse so they can eat it. Good for the ravens, hard on the horse.

Two repeated themes are notable: our old friend the Animal Helper, such as the ants who help Aschenputtel sort her lentils so she can go to the ball; and Transformation, where the animal is actually a human being under a spell, as in "The Frog Prince" and the haunting tale of "The Wild Swans." Here the demarcation of human and animal is so weak that one may become, may actually be, the other.

Ever since we lived in caves people have been calling other people greedy as a hog or brave as a lion. What is remarkable about "A Voyage to the Houyhnhnms" is not so much that Jonathan Swift used horses to provide a model of Enlightenment morality, but that he used humans, not animals, to satirize human vice. The honesty and dignity of the Houyhnhnms is not much exaggerated from that of ordinary horses, but they speak, and so are raised above the brute; while the Yahoos have no language, and no virtues, and so are sunk below any brute. Gulliver says, "I never beheld in all my travels so disagreeable an animal." Swift is careful never to compare the Yahoos to apes. If the Yahoos were mere apes they'd have an excuse for their nastiness. He wants us to see them as men, and we do.

Gulliver's Travels was not written for children, of course, and I don't know how many children these days get a chance to read it, abridged or entire. I think both the story and the satire of the third Voyage completely suitable to older children. Behind Swift's "savage indignation," after all, is the idealism that can conceive of so truthful and gentle a realm as that of the Houyhnhnms. (And any child who wants to know how to pronounce them can read T.H. White's *Mistress Masham's Repose* and find out.)

George Orwell's *Animal Farm* is a less complex satire, more straightforward in its stereotypes, therefore perhaps less disturbing to a young reader; but Orwell is in the end even harsher than Swift, for loyalty and honesty lose out in this modern fable, and whether the story is read as politically topical or as a general warning, its message is merciless.

The last animal satire I'll mention is one I have a little trouble thinking of as satirical, it is so sweet-natured, and perhaps all the stronger for that; I mean *The Story of Ferdinand*. When you come right down to it, Leaf is almost as hard on humans as Swift is, but a good deal more hopeful than Orwell. And is there any other satire in the world that ends, with no irony at all, "He is very happy"?

The last books in this section of Fables are two very different fantasies, a new one and an old one.

Philip Pullman's His Dark Materials trilogy is a long, richly imagined, and deeply incoherent work, in which I'll try only to trace the part animals play. Despite appearances, it is a small part.

The two cats in the story, who have a minor but important role, do what cats have often done in myth and fable: they cross between worlds. Otherwise they're just cats, realistically drawn. Animals are otherwise absent from the books, except for a tribe of polar bears who talk and build forts and use weapons, but who don't have daemons, as humans do.

Daemons are animals in form, and the reason why the trilogy—particularly the first volume—seems to be full of animals is that every human being has one. Until you reach puberty your daemon may take any animal shape at any moment; with your sexual maturity your daemon settles into a permanent form, always of the other gender. Social class is evidently a decisive influence: we are told that servants always have dog daemons, and see that upper-class people's daemons are rare and elegant creatures such as snow leopards. Your daemon accompanies you physically and closely at all times, everywhere; separation is unbearably painful. Though they do not eat or excrete, daemons are tangible, and you can pet and cuddle with your own daemon, though you must not touch anybody else's. Daemons are rational creatures and speak fluently with their owners and with others.

Wish-fulfilment is strong in this concept and gives it great charm: the ever-loyal, ever-present, dear companion, soulmate, comforter, guardian angel, and ultimately perfect pet: as with the beloved stuffed animal, you don't even have to remember to feed it.

But I think Pullman overloads the concept and then confuses it. He implies strongly that the daemon is a kind of visible soul, that to be severed from it is fatal; his plot hinges on the cruelty and horror of this separation. But then he begins changing the rules. We find that witches can live apart from their daemons; in the second volume we are in our world, where nobody has visible or tangible daemons; and, back in her world, the heroine Lyra leaves her daemon on the wharves of hell, and though she misses him, she lives on perfectly competently, and in fact saves the universe, without him. Their reunion seems almost perfunctory.

In a fantasy, to change or break your own rules is to make the story, literally, inconsequential.

If the daemons are meant to show that we are part animal and must not be severed from our animality, they can't do it. They aren't fitted for the job. The essence of animality is the body, the living body with all its brainless needs and embarrassing functions—exactly what the daemons do not have. They are spiritual beings, forms without substance. They are fragments or images of the human psyche given animal shape, wholly contingent, having no independent being and therefore incapable of relationship. Lyra's much-emphasized love for her daemon is self-love. In Pullman's world human beings are dreadfully alone, since his God has gone senile and there aren't any real animals. Except those two cats. Let us place our hope in the cats.

Through the Looking Glass begins with cats. Alice is talking to Dinah and her kittens, who don't talk back, so Alice does it for them, and then she climbs up onto the mantel piece with one of the kittens, and goes through the mirror… As noted before, cats cross between worlds.

The looking-glass world and the one down the rabbit hole are dreams, and therefore all the characters in them are aspects of Alice — again, fragments of psyche, but in a very different sense from Pullman's daemons. Contingent they may be, but their independence is notable. As soon as Alice gets through the glass into the garden, the flowers not only talk but talk back; they are extremely rude and passionate flowers. As in folktale, all creatures are on an equal footing, mingling and arguing, even turning into each other — the baby becomes a piglet, the White Queen a sheep — Transformation going both ways… Train passengers include humans, a goat, a beetle, a horse, and a gnat, which begins as a tiny voice in Alice's ear but presently is "about the size of a chicken." It asks if Alice dislikes all insects, and she replies, with admirable aplomb, "I like them when they can talk. None of them ever talk, where I come from."

Alice is a nineteenth-century British middle-class child with a tight, strict moral code of self-respect and respect for others. Her good manners are sorely tried by the behavior of the dream-creatures — whom we can see, if we choose, as acting out Alice's own impulses of rebellion, her passion, her wild wilfulness. Violence is not permitted; we know that the Queen's "Off with her head!" is a threat not to be executed. And yet nightmare is never far off. The creatures of Alice's dreams come close to total uncontrol, to madness, and she must wake to know herself.

The Alice books are not animal stories, but there is no way I could leave them out of this essay; they are the purest modern literary instance of the animals of the mind, the dream beasts that every human society has known as ancestors, as spirit-doubles, as omens, as monsters, and as guides. We have spiraled back round to the Dream Time, where human and animal are one.

This is a sacred place. That we got back to it by following a little Victorian girl down a rabbit hole is absolutely crazy and appropriate.

VIII. Conclusion

People and animals are supposed to be together.
We spent quite a long time evolving together,
and we used to be partners.

—Temple Grandin, *Animals in Translation*

We human beings have made a world reduced to our-selves and our artifacts, but we weren't made for it and have to teach our children to live in it. Physically and men-tally equipped to be at home in a richly various and un-predictable environment, competing and coexisting with creatures of all kinds, our children must learn poverty and exile, to live on concrete among endless human beings, seeing animals only as a bird high in the air, a beast on a leash or in a cage, a film image. But our innate, acute inter-est in animals as fellow beings, friend or enemy or food or playmate, can't be instantly eradicated; it resists depriva-tion. And imagination and literature are there to fill the void and reaffirm the greater community.

The themes I have picked out along the way support this idea. The Animal Helper motif of mutual aid across species, which we see in folktale and as clearly in modern animal stories, tells that kindness and gratitude can't be limited to your own species, that all creatures are kin.

Community is shown as fundamental, a given, by the assimilation of animal to human and the mingling as equals that we see in folktale and in such books as *The Wind in the Willows* and *Dr Dolittle*.

Transformation of man into beast, which in folktales is usually a curse or unhappy spell, in modern stories is more likely to be enlarging and educational, and even, as in the Wart's last great journey, to offer a glimpse of mystical participation, of an ultimate and eternal communion.

The yearning for a Lost Wilderness that runs through so many animal tales is a lament for the endless land-scapes and creatures and species that we have wasted and destroyed. These laments grow urgent, now. We come ever closer to isolating ourselves, a solitary species swarming on a desert world. "Look on my works, ye mighty, and despair."

We go crazy in solitude. We are social primates. Human beings need to belong. To belong to one another, first, of course; but because we can see so far and think so cleverly and imagine so much, we aren't satisfied by membership in a family, a tribe, people just like us. Fearful and suspicious as it is, the human mind yet yearns for a greater belonging, a vaster identification. Wilderness scares us because it is unknown, indifferent, dangerous, yet it is an absolute need to us; it is that animal otherness, that strangeness, older and greater than ourselves, that we must join, or rejoin, if we want to stay sane and stay alive.

The child is our closest link to it. The storytellers know that. Mowgli and young Wart reach out their hands, the right hand to us and the left hand to the jungle, to the wild beast in the wilderness, to the hawk and the owl and the panther and the wolf; they join us together. The six-year-old spelling out *Peter Rabbit*, the twelve-year-old weeping over *Black Beauty*—they have accepted what so much of their culture denies, and they too reach out their hands to rejoin us to the greater creation, keeping us where we belong.

Endnotes

[1]   White, *The Sword in the Stone*, p. 229.

[2]   For a thoughtful and thoroughly research-supported discussion of animal cognition, see Donald R. Griffin, *Animal Minds*, University of Chicago Press, 1992. Griffin shows how a rational wariness among biologists, zoologists, etc., about interpreting animal behavior in human terms, taken to irrational theoretical extremes, stultified scientific investigation of animal behavior for half the twentieth century. It still lingers on as a mindless dread of anthropomorphizing the animal subject—even when the subject happens to be an anthropoid, patiently signing from its cage, in ASL, "Let me out."

[3] Davison, *Red Heifer, a story of men and cattle*, p. 175.

[4] Ibid, p. 174.

[5] Ibid. p. 166.

[6] Salten, *Bambi, a Life in the Woods*, p. 125.

[6] Ibid. p. 126

[8] Ibid. p. 216.

[9] Ibid. p. 286.

[10] London, *White Fang*, p. 139.

[11] Ibid. p. 266.

[12] Seton, *The Biography of a Grizzly*, p. 117.

[13] Ibid. p. 106.

[14] Ibid. p. 91.

[15] Mukerji, *Gay-Neck : the story of a pigeon*, p. 6.

[16] Ibid. p. 69.

[17] Lindermann, *Stumpy*, p. 130.

[18] Adams, *Watership Down*, p. 256.

[19] Farley, *The Black Stallion*, p. 17.

[20] George, *Julie of the Wolves*, p. 59.

[21] Ibid. p. 59.

[22] Lofting. *Dr Dolittle*, p. 126.

[23] White, *The Sword in the Stone*, p. 33.

[24] Ibid. p. 305.

[25] Ibid. p. 306.

[26] Ibid. p. 311.

The Young Adult in the YA

This talk was written to deliver on the occasion of receiving the Margaret A. Edwards Award for young adult fiction from the American Library Association in 2004. When I whimpered that I did not know what my talk should be about, the librarians kindly suggested to me that nobody would mind if I talked about my work, so I tried to do that. The following year, needing a short talk for the Chicago Book Expo America, I raided this one, so you will find a few semi-duplicate paragraphs in "Some Assumptions About Fantasy."

IF anybody knows what Young Adult fiction is, it's you—this audience. I feel foolish trying to say anything about it to you. I tried writing vast generalities about Young Adult fiction and discovered that all I really know is what I do, insofar as I know what that is. The truth is, I just *did* Young Adult fiction without thinking about it. And it's very nice to be told by the Margaret Edwards Award that I did it satisfactorily. But I still don't know what it was I was doing.

How did I begin doing it? Unexpectedly. Herman Schein of Parnassus Press, who had published my mother's books for young children, wanted to publish books for older kids, and so he asked me to write one—a fantasy.

And I said, Oh no, no, I can't do that, I haven't written anything for children, don't know how, quite impossible, thank you very much, and ran away.

And I got home and rued my words. (Nobody can rue words more truly than a writer.) I'd never been asked to write a book. I'd submitted stories and novels for ten years to publishers who hadn't asked for them and didn't want them, and now, a *proposal?* Oh yes, yes! But no: I haven't written for kids, I have no idea what it involves, I don't like thinking about a specific audience, I refuse to put any restrictions on my imagination or vocabulary, and the stuff I want to write about isn't teen-age stuff. And a fantasy, he said. Like Tolkien? Oh my heavens! Compete with Shakespeare, sure! Forget it.

But thinking about Tolkien took my mind away to thinking about wizards...and so to something that had bothered me about wizards...Prospero, Merlin, Gandalf, all old. Peaked hat, white beard. Why? What were they before they were old beardy men? Young men—beardless. Kids. How did kids get to be old wizards? By being young wizards, evidently. Learning the craft, going to... wizard school?

Huh. Hey. *There's* an idea.

This is not a claim to have invented it. I plant no flags and do not pee on fences. In *The Sword in the Stone*, T.H. White has Merlin say something funny about going to wizard school, and I'm sure there are other predecessors. But, in 1968 nobody I knew of had worked the idea out.

And it took hold of me like a bulldog. No, more like a boa constrictor—it enwrapped and devoured me. I became it. This is what writing novels is like. Being an elephant living inside a boa constrictor. The Little Prince knew all about it.

The conception was not just of a school of magic, but of a child gifted with an essentially unlimited power who needs—urgently needs—to learn how to know and control such power. That is a big idea. It reverberates. It contains worlds.

So, a few months later the elephant emerged from the boa constrictor as *A Wizard of Earthsea*. Herman Schein was happy with it, and his wife Ruth designed its marvelous cover. And I was happy, too—I had a book I knew was closer to what I'd hoped to write than anything I'd yet written.

I think it was Herman who first said to me, don't worry about the vocabulary and the audience and all that: all a novel has to do to be Young Adult is have a protagonist over twelve and under twenty.

Is there anything else in fact that makes a YA a YA? It sounds like a rhetorical question, but it isn't; I really am asking you.

There may be other rules for the YA novel, and I may have even have followed them in my YA novels. Writers do a great many things of which they are not only unconscious but ignorant. Don't let the naïve fallacy of authorial omnipotence or the critical fallacy of authorial intent fool you for a minute. A book is planned, always, to some extent, and some books are very closely planned; but many of us fiction writers work in the dark, perhaps more than any other artists except poets, because we work with language inside the mind. We cannot be thinking about what we write as we write, because we are using the principle tool of thinking, language, to write with—and we have to use it for writing, not for thinking. We cannot be intellectually, articulately conscious of what we're doing as we write, any more than we can be intellectually, articulately conscious of the actual process and intent of typing on a keyboard while we type. To think about it consciously, in words, would stop us right there, fingers frozen above the keys—mind frozen above the plot.

And therefore, fiction writers learn, taoistically, to cherish our ignorance and trust it to do our job.

So long as we have been to wizard school.

We do have to learn the craft. That's all we have under our control and can use intentionally: craft. It takes us a long way. We are crafty people. The rest is gift.

So, whatever rules I was ignorantly following, the *Wizard* came out and was approved as a YA, taking my publisher rather by surprise at how it went on selling.

Now, here is an example of intentionality in book-planning: I had wondered why wizards were always not only whitehaired, but white men. (I wasn't ready yet to question the gender, only the color.) The only reason for the whiteness of wizards seemed to be that our fantasy tradition came largely from Northern Europe, with its weird skin-color hang-ups. So I just reversed the convention. My hero and all his people are reddish-brown to black, while the more villainous or barbaric types are white. Some readers notice this, many don't. Fine. I like my subversions to be more sneaky than preachy.

That was a deliberate, political decision, made "outside" the writing. Here, on the other hand, is an example of unintentionality, the stuff you write while you're following your story, "ignorantly," without knowing what it implies. A year or so after the *Wizard* came out, I was surprised to discover that it was full of hints of more to come. Right on the first page I had written about:

> the man called Sparrowhawk, who in his
> day became both dragonlord and Archmage.
> His life is told of in the Deed of Ged and
> in many songs, but this is a tale of the time
> before his fame, before the songs were made.

Now I'd thought this was just a crafty trick, learned mostly from Dunsany and Tolkien: the indication of time before the story and time after it and a great geography all around it, which gives the story a chance to reverberate.

But there was more to it than that. I had announced on the first page that Ged was a dragonlord and the Archmage. When I wrote that sentence I didn't know who Ged was, didn't know what an Archmage was, let alone a dragonlord.

So. How did he do that, how did he get there — what did those words mean?

I learned who he was and what archmages and dragonlords were by writing the first book; but Ged himself got there between books, while I wasn't watching. I was in the second book, looking away, looking east to the Kargad Lands, writing about a girl who, like him, had been given a terrible power, but unlike him wasn't taught rightly how to handle it.

People ask forever, where do you get your ideas from, and I have written several essays about it and still have no idea where I get my ideas from — except some of them. *The Tombs of Atuan* came directly from a three-day trip to eastern Oregon: the high desert, the high, dry, bony, stony, sagebrush and juniper country (just about as far as you can get from this soggy Florida). It wasn't the first time I'd seen desert, I am a Westerner after all, but it was the first time I had stayed in desert country, heard that silence, walked in twilight on that dangerous, infinitely fragile land. And driving home with the car full of kids and sweat and dust and twigs of sagebrush, I knew I was in love and had a book. The landscape gave it to me. It gave me Tenar and where she lived.

So the *Wizard* got a sequel; and soon I started the third book, *The Farthest Shore*, planning to follow Ged in it, and then a final one that would follow Tenar. Because my publishers — Atheneum by then — my splendid editor was Jean Karl — thought of the books as YA, I knew I had to have a young protagonist; but Earthsea had to have a king, too. So there you are. Young prince meets older wizard and they go sailing off together into death. Nothing to it.

So having found out what happened to Ged, I started on the fourth book, the one where I was to find out what happened to Tenar. I wrote a chapter, and stopped, because I didn't understand what was happening to Tenar. She had given up magic, she was a farmwife with a couple of kids. What was she thinking of?

It took me 17 years to find out. During those years, the second wave of feminism broke, and I learned how to write as myself, from the sensibility and intellect of a grown woman. That had not been the commonest thing in any genre, including realism; and fantasy had been particularly male-centered. It was a radical change. And a great one. I am lucky to have lived to see it and be part of it.

The key to my fourth book of Earthsea was not Tenar herself, but Therru, a young child who has been terribly used. When I saw that child I had my book. But Therru is not yet an adolescent and not even a protagonist, and everybody else in the story is middle-aged. Where is the obligatory teenager?

I have to confess I didn't worry about it. I'd grown up, my characters had grown up; if I thought about it I guess I thought, well, I hope my readers have grown up too. I went ahead and wrote the book I had to write. At the end the king was on his throne, the lovers were in each other's arms, and my private title for it was Better Late than Never. Publically I called *Tehanu* "the last book of Earthsea" because I thought it was. Oh idiot author.

It was met with some shrill accusations of man-hating feminism from people who think being a hero means you always win. But I guess most of my readers had indeed grown up, because they liked it fine. And I was happy again because I had brought my tale to its happy ending— ha, ha.

Again, omens and indications in the text, hints of story to come... And this time, to jog my obliviousness, letters from readers: Who is going to be the next Archmage? Who or what is Tehanu? What are the dragons?

And a huge blooper, which I had already realised with horror and hoped nobody would notice, but of course they did, though they were very kind and tactful about bringing it to my attention: the Master Summoner in the third book is dead; but in the fourth book he is alive and apparently well on Roke Island. Oh idiot idiot author!

Sometimes your mistake is your guide. I'd heard Rusty Schweikert the astronaut tell the tale of how when he went outside the space craft to do some external repair, he forgot a tool he needed, and while they were getting it to him, he had the first free time he had ever had on the mission—no programmed activity for five whole minutes. Hanging there on his lifeline in space, idle, because of a mistake, because of something he forgot, he had time to look around. And he looked, and he saw the Earth. The Earth his home, immense and fragile, shining there among the stars. A vision that changed his life forever.

That's a beautiful and useful learning story, and I used it. I looked at what I'd got wrong, and saw why it was wrong—because right wasn't quite what I'd thought it was.

By way of answering some of the questions I'd caused by absentmindedly reviving the dead, or had otherwise left unanswered, I wrote the various *Tales of Earthsea*, in which I finally established a coherent history. Certain features that, in 1968, I'd just bought wholesale from the heroic fantasy tradition—such as the supremacy and celibacy of male wizards—I had to really think about now, and explain, and fit into my Earthsea as I now perceived it, seen not only from the top, from the seats of power, but from below, through the eyes of the powerless, women and children, ordinary people. Some people think this change of view has led to a loss of enchantment in the stories. I don't. The last Tale led me straight into a nest of dragons. Soon after that, I wrote *The Other Wind*, which brings together all those questions: who Tehanu is; who the dragons are; and how, when clever people meddle with it through hubris or fear, death itself might go wrong.

There are young people in these last two books—Irian/Dragonfly, young Ogion, my dear Kargish Princess—but the books don't obey the teenage protagonist rule, and I don't think they're definably YA. Yet kids as well as adults seem to buy and read them, and I've had no protests so far about the advanced senility of Ged and Tenar. Why are the books thus forgiven?

Is it because they're fantasy? Is this a well-known fact, which I have just discovered with cries of Eureka!—that fantasy doesn't have to follow the YA rule, because it bridges the gaps between age-groups?

We read *Alice in Wonderland* or *The Wind in the Willows* first at eight, or earlier if they're read to us, and again at twelve, maybe, and again maybe every decade or so: and every time we read them we're a different person, yet each time, if we let them do it, they give us what is "appropriate to our age-group"—kiddies or mid-lifers or wrinklies. The *Jungle Books* contain stories that one may read happily at ten and understand with a hard jolt at forty-five. *Kim*, with its child/adolescent hero and its story that treads just on the edge of the fantastic, is a joy that only deepens with the decades. *The Once and Future King* is as magical, exasperating, fascinating, and moving to me now as it was when it was published. *The Hobbit* doesn't carry across the kid-to-adult gap reliably for everyone, but (going the other direction in Middle Earth) nine-year-olds are now reading *The Lord of the Rings*. Yet *The Lord of the Rings* is a fully adult book about fully adult concerns, with no children in it at all. Short adults, yes. But no kids.

So, the Edmund Wilsons of the world croak, what else is new? Fantasy is *all* infantile. Childish escapism. Mind-mush. Talking animals, elves, bushwa! I was charmed to learn that somebody said of Edmund Wilson that he always thought he was the only grown-up in the room. It is a common delusion of critics. It shouldn't be encouraged, but it can be ignored.

What should not be ignored is the curious capacity fantasy has of satisfying both the child and the adult—and even, most particularly, that creature of tormented and insatiable and uncomprehended and infinite needs and longings, the adolescent. How does fantasy do it? Or what does it do that none of the other genres including realism does?

Fantasy is the oldest form of literature. Even if storytelling began with Oog reciting to the family around the fire in the cave the true and factual story of How I Killed a Mammoth, you and I know that Oog's tale was not totally realistic. Elements of fantasy slipped in—the size of the mammoth, the length of the tusks, the intrepidity of Oog... It got better every time he told it. And after a couple of generations, maybe it was the tale of How Great

Hero Father Oog slew the Lord of the Mammoths, which is why we are the People of the Long Tusk—a legend, a myth. A work of the imagination. A fantasy.

They all begin in the same place, the place in our mind that knows what story is. What reality may be, what really happened, we cannot tell; what we can tell is the story, the infinitely flexible, wonderfully rearrangeable, extremely useful story. With it we remake reality. We remake it according to our desires and according to our needs. The truth of story is not fact. Neither is it wishful thinking. Story tells human truth, serving human community and spiritual longing. And the stories that call most on the imagination work on a deep level of the mind, beneath reason (therefore incomprehensible to rationalists), using symbol as poetry does to express what can't be said directly, using imagery to express what can't be perceived directly—using indirection to indicate the truthward direction.

And here myth and imaginative fiction run a risk; all fiction does, but it's particularly destructive to fantasy: the risk of being rationalised—interpreted, reduced to allegory, read as a message.

Such reduction is a nefarious act. Teachers and critics indulge in it with the best of motives, but they leave ruin in their wake. Fortunately, the strongest fantasies simply shrug off interpretation like a horse twitching off a fly. Everybody wants to tell us what *Alice in Wonderland* means, and the more they talk about Charles Dodgson and Victorian mores and mathematics and the libido, the farther they get from Lewis Carroll and Alice, who go on about their business on the chess board among the dodos, quite intact.

Take the currently almost unquestioned assumption that fantasy concerns a Battle Between Good and Evil. This assumption permits the author to declare one side good and the other bad without further inquiry as to what makes a person or an action good or evil. The heroes and the villains are equally arrogant, competitive, thoughtless, and bloody-minded, and so the Battle goes on till the Problem of Evil is solved in a final welter of violence and a win for the so-called Good team.

Being akin to legend and folktale and myth, with no necessary allegiance to modernism or realism or any limiting school of fiction, fantasy draws its scenery and characters and images and symbols from the whole range of human story-telling back to ancient times; and it doesn't have to clothe its people with distracting realistic trappings and contemporary disguises but can present them quite nakedly—the brave man, the kind woman, the mistreated child, the villain, the king, the traitor, the fool. Character is often less important in fantasy than role. To a careless reader such stark stuff may appear to be morally simplistic, black-and-white. And when it's carelessly written, that's what it is.

But careless reading of careful fantasy will not only miss nuance, it will miss the whole nature and quality of the work. Fantasy is in fact particularly suited to examining the *differences between* good and evil, both in act and in intent. The imagination is a powerful instrument of ethics. Imaginative literature offers the opportunity to test motive and behavior, to see how the unconscious may control the seemingly rational, to understand how the bravest deed may leave a track of ruin, to ask what the road to Hell is paved with, and why.

Americans think obsessively in terms of war and battle. The battle of life, the war between good and evil — these have always been suspect metaphors; in this time of ultimate weaponry they are actively dangerous. By glibly sanctioning violence as a solution, they prevent thought.

I don't write about wars between good and evil. What I write about — like most novelists — is people making mistakes, and people — other people or the same people — trying to prevent or correct those mistakes, while inevitably making more mistakes. The "problem of evil" in Earthsea is pretty much what it is here: that people don't or won't recognise the evil they do. In the first book, Ged doesn't know who he is, because he doesn't recognise his own shadow, the shadow we all cast.

Immature people crave and demand moral certainty: This is bad, this is good. Adolescents struggle to find a sure moral foothold in this bewildering world; they long to feel they're on the winning side, or at least a member of the Good team. To them, heroic fantasy may offer a vision of moral clarity. But a fictive battle between unquestioned Good and unexamined Evil is a mere excuse for violence — as brainless, useless, wasteful, and base as aggressive war in the real world. I hope that teenagers can struggle through these fakes to find the real heroic fantasies, like Tolkien's. I know such fantasies continue to be written. They don't have to be written for kids; kids will find them, whoever they're written for.

Which brings me to my final thought about Young Adult fiction. When I was in my teens, I certainly didn't feel that in order to interest me a book had to be about teenagers. I got enough of them at school, pimply creeps like me. I wanted to know about being grown up: and novels offered a chance to find out what that was like from inside. Kittens playing are playing cat.

So like all reading children who have the chance (which usually means the public library), I read way ahead of myself, blundering into Austen and Voltaire and Dostoyevsky and Dinesen and Dunsany and Steinbeck and Forster and you name it, understanding bits and not understanding lots; but that's how we learn to speak and read, isn't it?—by doing it: not word-by-word-exactly-correct, but with mistakes and misunderstandings, in bits and gulps and clumps that finally begin to stick together and make sense. Literature is a major tool for understanding the world and the life we have to live, and we learn to use it by using it.

The rule that the YA book should be about young adults may apply chiefly to the realistic novel of contemporary teen-age life and problems and to historical novels. In other genres, the adolescent reader doesn't seem to demand adolescent protagonists. That all the characters are adult doesn't stop a kid from reading *The Virginian*, or any other good Western; the Sherlock Holmes books, or any other good mystery; C.S. Forester, or Nordhoff and Hall, or Patrick O'Brian, or any other good sea story; or any science fiction story at all. Fantasy appeals to kids even earlier than the other genres, but much genre literature is like fantasy in this: once you're old enough to read it, it doesn't matter how old you *or* the characters are. Nine to ninety, as they say.

I suspect this whole talk has been an attempt to justify myself to myself for continuing the Young Adult trilogy of Earthsea with a trilogy of Old Adult Earthsea. But I have atoned! My next book, *Gifts*, is a YA with an unimpeachably, impeccably adolescent hero and hero-ine. Now, of course, I am thinking of following those two kids to find out what happens to them when they're thirty…but that is another story.

A Message about Messages

Written for the *Children's Book Council
Magazine*, Summer, 2005; slightly revised.

I MADE a note to myself a while ago: "Whenever they tell me *children want this sort of book* and *children need this sort of writing*, I am going to smile politely and shut my earlids. I am a writer, not a caterer. What children most want and need is what we and they don't know they want and don't think they need, and only writers can offer it to them."

Most fiction for kids and young adults is reviewed as if it existed in order to deliver a useful little sermon — "Growing up is tough but you can make it." "Popularity is not all it's cracked up to be." "Drugs are dangerous."

Does it ever occur to such reviewers that the meaning of the story might lie in the language itself, in the movement of the story as read, in an inexpressible sense of discovery, rather than a tidy bit of advice?

Readers — schoolkids and adults — constantly ask me to tell them "the message" of one story or another. I want to say to them: Your question isn't in the right language.

As a fiction writer, I don't speak *message*. I speak *story*.

Sure, my story means something, but if you want to know what it means, you have to ask the question in terms appropriate to story-telling. Terms such as "message" are appropriate to expository writing, didactic writing, sermons — different languages from fiction.

The notion that a story "has a message" assumes that it can be reduced to a few abstract words, neatly summarized in a school or college examination paper or a brisk critical review. If that were true, why would writers go to the trouble of making up characters and relationships and plots and scenery and all that? Why not just deliver the message? Is the story a box to hide an idea in, a fancy dress to make a naked idea look pretty, a candy coating to make a bitter idea easier to swallow? *Open your mouth, dear, it's good for you.* Is fiction decorative wordage concealing a rational thought, a message, which is its ultimate reality and reason for being?

A lot of teachers teach fiction, a lot of reviewers (particularly of children's books) review it, and so a lot of people read it, in that belief. The trouble is, it's wrong.

I'm not saying fiction is meaningless or useless. Far from it. I believe story-telling is one of the most useful tools we have for achieving meaning: it serves to keep our communities together by asking and saying *who we are*, and it's one of the best tools an individual has to find out who I am, what life may ask of me and how I can respond.

But that's not the same as having a message. The complex meanings of a serious story or novel can be understood only by participation in the language of the story itself. To translate them into a message or reduce them to a sermon distorts, betrays, and destroys them.

This is because a work of art is understood not by the mind only, but by the emotions and by the body itself.

It's easier to accept this about the other arts. A dance, a landscape painting—we're less likely to talk about its "message" than simply about the feelings it rouses in us. Or music: we know there's no way to say all a song may mean to us, because the meaning is not so much rational as deeply felt, felt through our emotions and by our whole body, and the language of the intellect can't fully express those understandings.

In fact, art itself is our language for expressing the understandings of the heart, the body, and the spirit.

Any reduction of that language into intellectual messages is radically, destructively incomplete.

This is as true of literature as it is of dance or music or painting. But because fiction is an art made of words, we tend to think it can be translated into other words without losing anything. So some people think a story is just a way of delivering a message.

And so kids ask me, in all good faith, "When you have your message, how do you make up a story to fit it?" All I can answer is, It doesn't work that way! I'm not an answering machine—I don't have a message for you! What I have for you is a story.

What you get out of that story, in the way of understanding or perception or emotion, is partly up to me—because of course the story is passionately meaningful to me (even if I only find out what it's about after I've told it). But it's also up to you, the reader. Reading is a passionate act. If you read a story not just with your head, but with your body and feelings and soul, the way you dance or listen to music, then it becomes your story. And it can mean infinitely more than any message. It can offer beauty. It can take you through pain. It can signify freedom. And it can mean something different every time you reread it.

I am grieved and affronted when reviewers treat my novels and other serious books for kids as candy-coated sermons. Of course there's a lot of moralistic and didactic stuff written for young people, which can be discussed as such without loss. But with genuine works of literature for children, with "The Elephant's Child" or *The Hobbit*, it is a grave error to teach or review them as mere vehicles for ideas, not seeing them as works of art. Art frees us; and the art of words can take us beyond anything we can say in words.

I wish our teaching, our reviews, our reading would celebrate that freedom, that liberation. I wish children in school, instead of being taught to look for a message in a story, were taught to think as they open the book, "Here's a door opening on a new world: what will I find there?"

Why Kids Want Fantasy,
or, Be Careful What You Eat

Published under the title "Questward Ho" in
Time Out New York Kids, June-Sept. 2004

FANTASY says that dragons exist, magic works, and cats can fly. It denies experience, defies possibility, and ignores gravity. Fantasy is transgressive — which may be the first reason why kids and teenagers love it.

Realism is an upstart kind of fiction that's been around only a couple of centuries and is already showing signs of senility. Fantasy has been here ever since we sat in the lodge and listened to the story of how Raven brought fire to the People. Its roots are in myth, legend, religious parable, the literatures that tell a people who they are. The *Iliad* and the *Odyssey* aren't realistic or historical; they're fantasies. So are the *Aeneid*, the *Mahabharata*, the *Tale of Monkey*. They all defy gravity, though not gravitas.

And as fantasy goes back to humanity's earlier days, so also in an individual life it's likely to be the earliest and most permanent experience of story. Where do we start? "There was an old woman who lived in a shoe…" *Goodnight Moon*… Talking locomotives, rabbits who drink tea, Cinderella, *The Story of Ferdinand* …

Fantasy is the native and natural form of children's story. Not because most kids don't know real from unreal, or need to "escape" from reality, but because their imaginations are working full time to make sense out of reality, and imaginative story is the best tool for doing just that job.

With any luck we're given our first fiction tool-kit early in life: nonsense rhyme and animal fable, folk tales and hero tales. Many of us go right on using them throughout life. Some will come to prefer realism. Some will stop reading fiction altogether, because reading is difficult for them, or their culture tells them fiction is unimportant, or contradicts scripture, or whatever. But at nine or ten, lucky kids start reading young adult and adult fantasy, and some will go on doing it the rest of their lives. Fantasy bridges the gap between child and adult as no other form of literature does.

Adolescents struggle fiercely and consciously to understand their world, make sense of it, cope with it, make moral choices. Their struggle is often genuinely desperate. They need help. Story is perhaps the most flexible tool at the disposal of mind. With it we remake reality. We retell events, we imagine alternatives, we figure out how to live according to our desires and according to our needs. The truth of story is not fact. Story tells human truth, serving ethical questioning, human community, and spiritual longing.

When they begin looking for a truth that works for them, a way that they can make for themselves into the dark wood of the world, kids often find it in fantasy — particularly if they're not content to take directions readymade from elders, teachers, and preachers, but seek their own direction. By training the imagination and opening alternatives, fantasy offers self-guidance. Imaginative literature of a high order offers guidance of a high order.

There is, of course, nothing childish about the great works of fantasy. But even now people say with preening self-congratulation "Of course *I* don't read that sort of thing," that sort of thing being Tolkien.

The real, constant, damn-the-critics popularity of *The Lord of the Rings,* and the increase in number and quality of other non-modernist and po-mo nonrealistic fiction, including magical realism, finally showed the irrelevance of modernist dogma to what is—and always was—actually going on. It may be that the greatest fictional legacy of the twentieth century, from Kafka to Borges, from Tolkien to Saramago, will turn out to be—well, call it what you will, but realism it ain't.

However...

Nothing fails like success.

Fantasy has become a big commercial genre. All you need is a map with weird names. Everybody has a sword and does sorcery, there is no known basis to the economy, and the obligatory War Between Good and Evil is going on. The Good guys and the Evil guys are hard to tell apart since all of them use violence as the response to all situations and the solution to all problems. The Good guys are the ones that win in the third volume of the trilogy.

Fantasy films used to be rare, and mostly animation, because it was difficult to build dragons. Now it's just a flick of the old industrial magic and there's your dragon.

But is he a real one, or a fake? Real dragons can destroy you, and they keep a jewel in their hoard, called wisdom. Fake dragons don't. Fake dragons never get out of the box office.

Meaningless imitation, formula repetition, is always the problem when a genre has mastered its techniques and refined its subject matter. That doesn't matter to the producers of fantasy-by-the-yard; it makes it all the easier for them to produce it. But the stuff they make is shoddy, a fabric that comes to pieces at once.

I recommend caution to both adults and children entering what used to be called Fairyland. Take care. It always was a dangerous place. Wisdom is not easy to come by, and never cheap. Be careful what you eat. Beware of sorcerers who lead you astray by false arts. You'll come out onto the cold hillside and find the money in your pocket has turned to dead leaves and your hair is grey.

But if you seek true guides into the lands of fantasy, if you follow the real wizards, you may not get rich, or stay young, or win any Battle between Good and Evil, but you'll learn something about how to tell the *difference* between good and evil. And that knowledge is the Arkenstone, the jewel of jewels.

Sources of Illustrations

Page number in current volume is followed by description of illustration and page number in original publication.

Black Beauty: the autobiography of a horse by Anna Sewell. New York: Grosset & Dunlap, 1945.

56:     Liberty, p. 29

Forgotten Children's Books, assembled by Andrew W. Tuer, Ondgon: The Leadenhall prefs, Ltd. 1898-9.

19:     Squirrel with spider, p. 147

104:    Cat, p. 505

125:    Bull, p. 495

129:    Cattle, p. 500

131:    Moth with knight, p. 477

The Oxford Nursery Rhyme Book, assembled by Iona and Peter Opie. New York and Oxford: Oxford University Press. 1955

3:      Owl from *The Story Teller*, London: J Harris and Soon, 1822, p. 97

52:     Owl from *History of British Birds*, vol. i, The figures
        engraved on wood by t. Berwick. p. 67

136:    Bat. p. 74. From *Aesop's Fables.* Buglin: W. Espy. 1824

The Jungle Book by Rudyard Kipling. Illustrated by
        J.L. Kipling, W.H. Drake, and P. Frenzenzy.
        London and New York: Macmillan and Co. 1894.

8:      Nagina, Rikki-Tikki, p. 147

42:     Elephant and boy, p. 156

85:     White Seal, p. 95

107:    Animal/human frieze, p. 32

The Second Jungle Book by Rudyard Kipling. Illustrated by J.L.
        Kipling.
        London and New York: Macmillan and Co. 1894

iv: Triangle motif with bear and child, p. 22

ix: Deer with antlers, p. 46

48:     Illustrated Y, p. 48

135:    Animal/human frieze, p. 210

Just So Stories by Rudyard Kipling. Illustrated by
        Rudyard Kipling.
        Garden City, NY: Doubleday Page & Co., 1925.

72:     Cat, p. 207

Cheek by Jowl

Bibliography

Adams, Richard. *Watership Down*. Rex Collings, 1972; New York: Puffin Books, 1973.

Alexander, Caroline. *Mrs. Chippy's Last Expedition: the remarkable journal of Shackleton's polar-bound cat*. New York: HarperCollins Publishers, 1997.

Andersen, H. C., Neil Philip, and Sally Holmes. *The Snow Queen: A Story in Seven Parts*. New York: Lothrop, Lee & Shepard Books, 1989.

Ashmore, Marion. *Lost, Stolen, or Strayed: the adventures of an Aberdeen terrier*. London: Eyre and Spottiswoode, 1931; New York: Scribner's, 1931.

Attebery, Brian. *Strategies of Fantasy*. Bloomington, IN: Indiana University Press, 1992.

Bagnold, Enid. *National Velvet*. New York: W. Morrow, 1949.

Baum, L. Frank. *Dorothy and the Wizard of in Oz*. Chicago: Reilly & Britton Co., 1908. Maybe don't need to include one of the Oz books, or maybe this first one would be good to acknowledge.

Bernheimer, Kate, ed. *Mirror, Mirror on the Wall: Women Writers Explore their Favorite Fairy Tales*. New York: Anchor Books, 1998.

Bloom, Harold. *The Anxiety of Influence; a theory of poetry*. New York: Oxford University Press, 1973.

Burnford, Sheila. *The Incredible Journey.* Boston: Little, Brown, 1961.

Carroll, Lewis, and Gertrude Welling. *Alice in Wonderland, And Through the Looking Glass*. New York: J.H. Sears & Co, 1926.

Carroll, Lewis, and John Tenniel. *Through the Looking-Glass and What Alice Found There*. New York: Macmillan, 1926.

Clement-Davies, David. *Fire Bringer*. London: Macmillan Childrens Books, 1999; New York: Dutton Books, 2000.

Clutton-Brock, T. H., F. E. Guinness, and S. D. Albon. *Red Deer: Behavior and Ecology of Two Sexes. Wildlife behavior and ecology*. Chicago: University of Chicago Press, 1982.

Craighead George, Jean *Julie of the Wolves.* Pictures by John Schoenherr. New York: Harper & Row, 1972.

Darling, F. Fraser. *A Herd of Red Deer; A Study in Animal Behavior*. London: Oxford University Press, H. Milford, 1937.

Davison, Frank Dalby. *Red Heifer, a story of men and cattle.* Introduction by Kermit Roosevelt; illustrated by Frank Wallace. New York, Coward-McCann, 1934 (1935 printing). (Won Australian Literary Society Gold Medal for Best Australian Novel, 1934.)

de Saint-Exupéry, Antoine. *The Little Prince*. New York: Harcourt, Brace, & World, 1943.

Farley, Walter. *The Black Stallion*. Illustrated by Keith Ward. New York: Random House, 1941; New York: Knopf Bullseye Books, 1991.

Grahame, Kenneth. *The Wind in the Willows*. New York: Charles Scribner's Sons, 1908.

Griffin, Donald R. *Animal Minds*, Chicago, IL: University of Chicago Press, 1992.

Grimm, Jacob, Wilhelm Grimm, and Mervyn Laurence Peake. *Household Tales*. London: Methuen, 1973.

————.*Household Stories, from the Collection of the Bros. Grimm.* Translated by Lucy Crane. Macmillan 1886, Dover 1963.

Gipson, Fred. *Old Yeller*. New York : Perennial Library, 1964.

Henry, Marguerite, and Wesley Dennis. *Misty of Chincoteague*. New York: Junior Literary Guild, 1947.

Hoban, Russell. *The Mouse and His Child*, 1967, Scholastic Ed. 2000.

Jacques, Brian, and Gary Chalk. *Redwall*. New York: Philomel Books, 1986.

James, Will. *Smoky, the Cowhorse*. New York: Scribner, 1926.

Kipling, Rudyard. *Jungle Books. (I and II)* Garden City, NY: Doubleday, 1948. (Original: 1894, 1895.)

————. *Just So Stories.* Garden City, NY: Doubleday Page & Co., 1925.

————. *Kim.* London: MacMillan, 1901.

Kroeber, Karl. *Romantic Fantasy and Science Fiction*, New Haven, CT: Yale University Press, 1988.

Leaf, Munro. *The Story of Ferdinand.* New York: Viking Press, 1938.

Linderman, Frank B. *Stumpy*. Illustrated by H.M. Stoops. Chicago: E.M. Hale, 1933.

Lockley, R. M. *The Private Life of the Rabbit: An Account of the Life History and Social Behaviour of the Wild Rabbit.* London: Corgi, 1976.

Lofting, Hugh. *The Story of Doctor Dolittle*. New York: Lippincott, 1920.

————. *The Voyages of Doctor Dolittle.* Illustrated by Sonja Lamut. New York: Grosset & Dunlap, 1998

London, Jack. *White Fang*. New York: Macmillan Pub. Co., 1933-1934.

MacDonald, George. *At the Back of the North Wind*. Collins, 1958.

Morey, Walt, and John Schoenherr. *Gentle Ben*. New York: Dutton, 1965.

Mukerji, Dhan Gopal. *Gay-Neck : the story of a pigeon.* Illustrated by Boris Artzybasheff. New York: E.P. Dutton, 1927; Dutton Children's Books, 1954.

O'Brien, Robert C., and Zena Bernstein. *Mrs. Frisby and the Rats of Nimh*. New York: Atheneum, 1971.

Orwell, George. *Animal Farm*. New York: Harcourt, Brace, 1954.

Potter, Beatrix. *The tale of Peter Rabbit*. London: Strangeways, 1902.

Pullman, Philip. *The Amber Spyglass*. New York: Alfred A. Knopf, 2000.

————. *The Golden Compass*. New York: Alfred A. Knopf; Distributed by Random House, 1996.

————. *The Subtle Knife*. New York: Knopf, 1997.

Salten, Felix, and Whittaker Chambers. *Bambi, a Life in the Woods*. New York: Simon and Schuster, 1928.

Seton, Ernest Thompson. *The biography of a grizzly and 75 drawings*. New York: Schocken Books, 1967.

Sewell, Anna. *Black Beauty: the autobiography of a horse.* New York: Grosset & Dunlap, 1945.

Swift, Jonathan. *Gulliver's Travels.* edited with an introduction by Paul Turner. World's Classics. New York: Oxford University Press, 1998.

———.*Gulliver's travels : based on the 1726 text: contexts, criticism.* edited by Albert J. Rivero. 1st ed. Norton critical edition. New York: Norton, 2002.

Terhune, Albert Payson. *Lad: a Dog.* New York: E.P. Dutton & Co, 1926.

Todorov, Tzvetan. *The fantastic; a structural approach to a literary genre.* Cleveland: Press of Case Western Reserve University, 1973.

Tolkien, J. R. R., and Christopher Tolkien. *The Monsters and the Critics, and Other Essays.* London: Allen & Unwin, 1983.

Tolkien, J. R. R. *The Hobbit: Or, There and Back Again.* New York: Ballantine Books, 1965.

———. *The Fellowship of the Ring: Being the First Part of The Lord of the Rings.* Boston: Houghton Mifflin Co, 1965.

———. *The Two Towers; Being the Second Part of The Lord of the Rings.* Boston: Houghton Mifflin, 1965.

———. *The Return of the King: Being the Third Part of The Lord of the Rings.* Boston: Houghton Mifflin Co, 1965.

Warner, Sylvia Townsend. *Collected Poems.* New York: Viking Press, 1983.

White, E. B., Garth Williams, and Edith Goodkind Rosenwald. *Charlotte's Web.* New York: Harper, 1952.

White, T. H. *Mistress Masham's Repose.* New York: G.P. Putnam's Sons, 1946.

————. *The Once and Future King.* New York: Putnam, 1958.

————. *The Sword in the Stone.* With decorations by the author and end papers by Robert Lawson. New York, G. P. Putnam's sons, 1939.

Author Biography

Starting in 1929, Ursula Kroeber grew up in Berkeley (school year) and the Napa Valley (summer). She unexpectedly went East to college at Radcliffe, unexpectedly got a Fullbright while in grad school at Columbia, and unexpectedly fell in love with another Fullbrighter, Charles Le Guin, and married him in Paris. Their three children were not entirely unexpected, though, like all children, immensely surprising, having turned into a cellist, an English professor, and a market researcher, and furnished four grandchildren, all of whom are surprising. The only thing she ever fully expected to do was write, which she has done.

After ten years of sending out poetry and fiction and getting a few poems published, Ursula K. Le Guin finally got a story published in a literary magazine and a story in a science-fiction magazine, almost simultaneously. The fact that the sf magazine was able to pay (thirty dollars!) influenced her to submit more stories to more sf publishers. Having established a reputation with the novels *The Left Hand of Darkness* and *A Wizard of Earthsea*, and won some prizes, she was able to branch out again and publish work both within the sf, fantasy, and kiddilit genres and outside them, and has continued to do so. This freedom suits her inclination to do the unexpected in a kind of quiet, sneaky way.

Although *Left Hand* was one of the first novels to put gender directly in question, the first three Earthsea books were fairly conventional about male and female roles, though reversing the skin-color convention usual in fantasy; the last three, written some two decades later, deconstruct gender and power issues also. *The Dispossessed* and *Always Coming Home* are utopian novels, the second more adventurous in technique and idea. *Orsinian Tales* and *Searoad* collect her stories, many of which were published in *The New Yorker*, about an invented Central European country and the Oregon coast. In the last few years she has published three fantasy novels, *Gifts*, *Voices*, and *Powers*, and a novel, *Lavinia*, developed from a character in Vergil's *Aeneid*. She has published seven volumes of poetry. A full bibliography, list of awards, and so on can be found at her website, ursulakleguin.com. She continues to write (mostly poetry at the moment) and to find life unexpected.